SUCCESSFUL PROJECT MANAGEMENT

SUCCESSFUL PROJECT MANAGEMENT

TREVOR L YOUNG

CREATING SUCCESS

KoganPage

Publisher's note

Every possible effort has been made to ensure that the information contained in this book is accurate at the time of going to press, and the publishers and author cannot accept responsibility for any errors or omissions, however caused. No responsibility for loss or damage occasioned to any person acting, or refraining from action, as a result of the material in this publication can be accepted by the editor, the publisher or the author.

First published in 2000 by Kogan Page Limited
Second edition 2006
Third edition 2010
Fourth edition 2013

120 Pentonville Road	1518 Walnut Street, Suite 1100	4737/23 Ansari Road
London N1 9JN	Philadelphia PA 19102	Daryaganj
United Kingdom	USA	New Delhi 110002
www.koganpage.com		India

© Trevor L Young, 2000, 2006, 2010, 2013

The right of Trevor L Young to be identified as the author of this work has been asserted by him in accordance with the Copyright, Designs and Patents Act 1988.

ISBN   978 0 7494 6720 3
E-ISBN   978 0 7494 6721 0

British Library Cataloguing-in-Publication Data

A CIP record for this book is available from the British Library.

Library of Congress Cataloging-in-Publication Data

Young, Trevor L. (Trevor Leonard), 1940-
  Successful project management / Trevor L Young. – 4th Edition.
    pages cm
  ISBN 978-0-7494-6720-3 – ISBN (invalid) 978-0-7494-6721-0 (ebk.)   1. Project management.   2. Time management.   I. Title.
  HD69.P75Y69 2013
  658.4'04–dc23   2012045497

Typeset by Graphicraft Limited, Hong Kong
Printed and bound by Ashford Colour Press Ltd, Gosport, Hampshire

CONTENTS

The project process – key steps for success 45

Project conception and start-up 54

The definition phase 84

Managing the stakeholders   102

Managing the risks   116

Planning the project 135

Launching and executing the project 166

Closure and post-project evaluation 201

INTRODUCTION

In the prevailing climate of restraint and difficult marketing conditions for all types of business, many are faced with changing the way they operate to remain effective and profitable. Without these changes many businesses are looking at potential failure and yet many managers and directors do not have the necessary skills to establish a strategy and achieve the changes necessary to turn potential failure into success.

So how can this book help you? It is now well established that change can only happen effectively through the use of the skills of project management. The tools and processes that are well proven in engineering projects have been shown to be extremely useful in all types of business and all types of projects. Here we will explore the steps you can take to significantly raise the probability of success with your projects. The contents are therefore aimed at managers who are concerned about getting the right results from projects in their organizations and project managers who are responsible for one or more projects.

This demands a starting point that is based on a simple but highly significant presumption – that you already have experienced the difficulty of creating and making changes work. This may have been called a 'project' or an 'initiative'. You may have considered your last project to end with a successful conclusion and you are now seeking ways to improve that success by degrees. Perhaps you are aware of the possibility of improving the degree of success to ensure the results are received with greater acclaim. Or you may have been less fortunate and involved in a project that has been labelled a failure by someone. It is a common experience that once a project is called anything less than a success by someone, the story becomes legend even if it is not true. Perceptions of failure spread like electricity down the wire and everyone knows why success was eluded while many will forecast your future!

HOW TO USE THIS BOOK

Of course success in any venture is never guaranteed. The steps towards achieving success are vulnerable to many factors. Many are predictable and some are not so easy to predict. The objective is to help you with a practical approach to improve the way you start and conduct your next project to overcome some of the factors that impede success. Although this assumes some basic understanding of the formal processes used in project management, where appropriate the relevant processes that are key to achieving success are explained in more detail with guidelines for their application in the project process.

- Chapter 1 discusses the perceptions of success and how we define success with projects.
- Chapter 2 outlines the importance of creating an appropriate climate for success and the roles and responsibilities for this climate to generate success with all the projects.
- Chapter 3 identifies the project process phases and key steps for success.
- Chapters 4 and 5 concentrate on the initial conception and definition phases of the project.
- Chapter 6 specifically looks at how to manage the stakeholders, a key step for success.
- Chapter 7 discusses how to manage risks in the project, another significant key step for success.
- Chapters 8–10 concentrate on the planning, execution and closure phases of the project.

KEY FACT

Throughout the book you will find Key facts. These are important facts that need to be accepted by everyone involved in project work. Stress them to your team members with constant reminders as the underlying principles of project management. Many highlight the need for action by someone if a successful outcome is to be achieved.

CHECKLISTS

Throughout the book you will find Checklists to help you through specific activities in the project management process. These are generalized based on experience in many types of project. Build them yourself based on your experience and add checkpoints or additional questions specific to your type of project and business. This will help you become a more effective project manager and add to your chances of success.

A NEW WAY OF WORKING?

To adopt the processes given here may require you to change the way you work and set aside some of those practices that have become habits for you. Changing your habits is never easy to accept as a necessity, particularly as you believe your working practices have served you well up to now. Such a conflict makes you feel uncomfortable because you are entering an area of low experience. All the processes and techniques discussed in this book are proven, practical ways to help you. It will be to your advantage to learn them and find a way to apply them in your situation.

Throughout the book you will find examples of standardized data recording formats that have been well tested. Accurate and organized data recording is an essential element of success and this is discussed in more detail in Chapter 4. If you use project management software some of these forms will be included.

Everything discussed here can be applied to any type of project irrespective of the nature of your business and regardless of whether your customer is internal or external to your organization. Finally you will find a glossary of terms used and some additional reading when project work has really attracted your attention for future development.

WHAT IS SUCCESS?

When a major project is perceived as a failure, someone will take up the challenge the organization faces to avoid a repeat. This evaluation may be prompted by a new product or service being late to market, customer needs not being satisfied or even a realization that a large sum of money has been expended with little or no chance of any return on the investment made. The result could be a question of organizational survival in a highly competitive market environment if there is a succession of failures. The initial focus of the evaluation in such situations is nearly always the degree to which project management skills were understood and employed during the project time span. Then it is often seen that the project manager and the team have done all the right things at the right time within the project.

Yet something clearly went wrong somewhere and a wider view is taken to identify the cause. Then it becomes more obvious that project management competencies and skills alone are no guarantee of success. Many parts of any organization have a strong influence on every project initiated and an understanding of project management and the processes used must be part of everyone's learning today in all departments, not just the project team.

WHAT HAPPENS TO THE PROJECT?

Someone identifies an opportunity for some new business, somewhere in the organization. A project team is assembled and a project manager assigned. The team may be assembled with individuals from all or just one or two of these departments. The Management Information System is designed to help run the business, not projects, yet this opportunity may be perceived by a few people as a vital element of future survival for the business. The project is conducted in a virtual envelope and when it looks as if it might have a 'successful outcome', the Manufacturing department is informed. Then it is discovered that the project team made some wrong assumptions and capital expenditure is required. Perhaps forward manufacturing plans to meet the order book have no capacity to run tests and pilot samples for at least six months. The Sales department get wind of what is happening and start shouting for the new product and major conflicts arise as every department highlights its own needs, to avoid making changes now and accommodate the project team. The consequence is demotivation of the project team, as no one appears to have clear responsibility for getting decisions made to promote the outputs from the project team.

How often does this type of situation develop with projects? This is a constant risk associated with project work if the projects in an organization are treated as something separate and disconnected with the normal day-to-day operations of the business.

How can this be corrected in the real world? The climate in which the projects are conducted has to be created with the active involvement of all the departments, some of which may initially think they have no part to play in the project. There are few projects in any organization today that do not involve, influence or affect many or all departments. Managers of these departments and the senior management of the organization cannot afford to risk ignoring the project activities that they consider do not affect them. They may not initially see any linkage between their activities and the project, or consider the project is a waste of valuable money and resource effort. Or the project may become the pawn in a political game as managers individually express open support, cynicism or opposition to the project to fit their own personal agendas.

DEFINING SUCCESS

Success is one of those words that conjure up a picture we paint in our minds. What sort of picture do you see for success? Is it huge financial gain, public recognition, promotion to senior management or just a great personal internalized feeling of achieving something you had initially determined was something to attain?

YOUR VIEW OF SUCCESS

EXERCISE

Think about the projects you have either led as a project manager, in which you have been a team member or even those where you have been merely an uninvolved observer. Now try to put into words how you would describe a successful project: 'My idea of a successful project is characterized by...'

COMMENTS

If we look in the dictionary for a definition of success we find it defined as 'attainment of object, or of wealth, fame or position' with synonyms such as victory, accomplishment, achievement, prosperity, attainment, fruition, winning. In a project environment this raises some questions:

1 Do any of these words appear in your description of the picture you have painted above?
2 For all those projects where you have some direct experience, how many fit your description?
3 Does the word 'customer' appear in your description of success?
4 Have you included some means of measuring a successful outcome?
5 Does your description include some measurement of time-related benefit?

Now ask some of your colleagues if their view is the same. Explore how their perception of success varies from your view. You will agree on some characteristics and differ on others because perceptions of success are driven by individual beliefs about what was expected as the outcomes from any project. If these expectations are not satisfied then the project is labelled as only a partial success. A partial success often becomes perceived as a failure just because some of these expectations were not satisfied. Ask some senior managers for their views on the same projects and discover if there is any variance with your view.

SUCCESS DEPENDS ON WHO IS MEASURING

Clearly the perception of success is dependent on who has established some metrics and is then making the measurements. All projects characteristically feature some specific roles:

- *The customer* – the 'purchaser' of the project outcomes or results. This individual may be internal or external to the organization and represent the 'end users' of these outcomes. The customer may be viewed as the individual who demanded the project initially or became engaged or involved after the project was completed. There may be several customers with different needs leading to a range of requirements for the project.

- *The sponsor* – the individual inside the organization who has accountability for the project. The sponsor drives the project in the right direction to benefit the organization.

- *The project manager* – the individual who has the day-to-day responsibility for the project work and is charged with completing this work on time, to an agreed budgeted cost and quality.

- *The project team* – the people who carry out all the tasks planned in the project schedule.

- *The resource managers* – the departmental managers who have direct responsibility for the people you seek to engage in your project team to complete the project work. These team members may be part-time on your project, work on other projects concurrently or be dedicated full-time to your project for a fixed time period.

Each of these individuals separately or collectively in groups has different reasons for qualifying and defining success. Conversely they can usually very quickly give you an opinion on failure or advise you what will lead to failure. Just how each can contribute to success or failure is key to your management of the project. As we examine each of the key steps to achieving success we will take a look at the actions you can take to avoid failure and enable a successful outcome.

WHAT ARE THE PERCEIVED CAUSES OF FAILURE?

Many reasons are quoted for projects failing in organizations. Some of the more common reasons quoted, often in combination are given as:

- Poor definition of objectives at the outset.
- Inability to build a truly cross functional team.
- Lack of understanding of team member availability and capacity to do the work.
- Inadequate schedule management leading to schedule creep – elastic schedules.
- Weak leadership.
- Lack of senior management commitment.
- Minimizing complexity with consequent technical problems not resolved.
- Inability to anticipate problems.
- Poor planning and control – the feeling that planning is an unnatural act.
- Too many uncontrolled changes with consequent scope creep.
- Resistance to change.
- Inadequate resources.
- No effective communication process.
- Assumed knowledge, skills and experience of team members.
- Scope not clear or controlled as project progresses.
- Confused roles and responsibilities – who does what when?
- 'I'll do it my way' (great song because my part's okay, but lousy management).
- Titanic complex – 'This project is sponsored by the MD and is unsinkable' so no one is looking for icebergs!

- Speed is only for Formula One racing junkies – we'll take as long as it takes.

- Over-optimism about time due to our innate ability to underestimate everything.

- All projects here are runaway trains – once started they just keep on going.

- We've done enough. Let's declare victory and go home.

- We didn't even have to involve the customers – we just told them after we finished.

- Success criteria? What are they?

REDUCE THE PROBABILITY OF FAILURE

The watch for potential failure is a continuous activity that must be a responsibility of everyone involved not just the project manager. Risk management processes are an essential and integral part of project management and will help reduce the probability of failure. Creating the platinum version of the product or service is ambitious and often more complex. Of course the team are having fun, justifying their existence and sustaining their continued employment!

It is easy for the team to convince themselves that providing a feature rich product or service is obviously going to be seen by the customers as more beneficial eventually. In reality you continue to do this development with a high risk that a competitor will take the business well before your organization, reducing your potential market share. Grabbing a competitor's market share is never an easy path to follow. The reduction of the probability of failure must, therefore, take a wider view than just the internal activities of the team and their project work.

THE CLIMATE FOR SUCCESS

In every organization today there is always a list of systems, processes, services and products that need to be improved, modified or even introduced to make the business more secure and grow. Unfortunately the resulting enduring benefits these changes promised have not always been successful in sustaining and growing the business.

In many organizations the mention of 'initiative' creates an immediate adverse reaction in the staff: 'Not another one!' Senior management has frequently failed to recognize that their role does not end when the initiative is framed, written down and published. They will even commit huge sums of money to provide training and internal publicity and then believe that it will then just happen. Worse still the senior management believe that because they have endorsed the initiative it is happening when in reality it has gone sadly wrong. When challenged they are unable to explain why the benefits did not accrue and will use excuses like: 'It was the wrong time to do something like that in this organization.' The cost may run into millions every year and even result in closure and release of a complete workforce.

WHY DO INITIATIVES APPEAR TO FAIL?

Some should never have started but are driven by what is fashionable in the prevailing business environment. Some are introduced by whim alone and no real study of the need and real analysis of the expected outcomes and benefits.

A large number fail to have any real impact because the organization:

- has no discipline in following processes demanded by the initiative
- has existing embedded processes that conflict with new processes
- does not understand how to introduce and control changes
- has not matured a 'global' approach to managing change
- has no shared clarity of strategy that drives decision making processes.

An appropriate climate for success needs to be established and this does require specific actions by the organization leadership to create the best environment to avoid failure.

SOME DEFINITIONS

Most initiatives have common elements that provide the organization with an opportunity to:

- Grow the business through developing ideas linked to long and short term strategy
- Develop, learn and acquire new skills and knowledge
- Demonstrate a high profile way to initiate new developments of products or services
- Create more effective or new working practices
- Improve performance and customer relationships

All of these activities are essential properties of projects and programmes so let us introduce some important definitions:

DEFINITION

A PROJECT is a temporary endeavor to achieve some specific objectives in a defined time.

Projects may vary considerably in size and duration, involving a small group of people or large numbers in different parts of the organization, even working in different countries. The desired outcomes are unique and will never be repeated even though many of the included activities are common to different projects.

DEFINITION

PROJECT MANAGEMENT is a dynamic process that utilizes the appropriate resources of the organization in a controlled and structured manner to achieve some clearly defined objectives identified as strategic needs. It is always conducted within a defined set of constraints.

Many organizations have now realized that *project management* includes a skill set ideal for the management of change. Since projects are about creating something or a state we need but do not have, then it is the obvious management process to adopt when an organization is faced with significant change.

In many situations we see the need for more than one project to achieve the final outcome desired. In larger projects it is often convenient to divide the work involved into a collection or 'suite' of projects across an organization, particularly where different national cultures or complex structures may have an influence. Sometimes in technical projects a specific department may have all the skills required and this makes implementation easier to accomplish. Additionally some projects in the suite may take longer than others and spread over more than one accounting year. For these and numerous other reasons we introduce the concept of Programmes.

DEFINITION

A PROGRAMME is a collection of inter-dependent projects, managed in a co-ordinated manner that together will provide the desired outcomes. Programmes are usually phased with target end dates of the initial phases well defined and committed and subsequent phases are defined as the initial phase approaches completion, enabling new related projects to be initiated.

Whenever there are several projects involved with phasing over a period of time then we use *programme management* to manage and control the change process. It is common for one project to subsequently be divided into several smaller projects creating a programme.

DEFINITION

PROGRAMME MANAGEMENT is the utilization of project management and its inherent processes to manage a collection of closely inter-dependent projects in a controlled and structured manner to achieve some clearly defined objectives identified as strategic needs.

The processes employed for programmes and projects are similar.

KEY FACT

Programme and Project management is industry independent – the skills and techniques developed over the past 50 years have been proven as valid for any type of business to assist in achieving strategic objectives

Neither addresses the key issue of what the organization is striving to achieve in strategic terms. To solve this issue we need to introduce the concept of *portfolio management* to relate the initiatives to the organization strategy.

DEFINITION

PORTFOLIO MANAGEMENT is concerned with managing all active programmes and projects along with future opportunities to ensure the resources of the organization are deployed in the most effective manner to achieve strategic objectives.

Strategic objectives in any organization are usually set at the highest level and cascade down the organization structure. Many of these will lead to defined short- and long-term strategies that generate projects focused on supporting the development and growth of the business with new services, products or systems to serve the market place.

KEY FACT

Portfolio management is the key process enabling success with all the active and proposed programmes and projects in an organization where these initiatives represent a change from the prevailing situation.

Generally we will address projects in this book although much of the content applies equally to programmes, since these are really just much larger projects with some additional characteristics.

PROJECTS – ARE THEY JUST AN ACCIDENT?

Project management has been called the 'accidental profession'. One of the most common ways to drop into the role is to identify a significant problem or business opportunity and then be told to pull a project team together to deal with the problem or opportunity. You then find that this is really a way of keeping you well overloaded with work. If you are successful you hand the manager who gave you the role initially an opportunity of demonstrating their ability to predict business or customer needs and gain kudos for their forward vision and justify their position. If the 'project' fails the consequence is never mentioned again and life in your department continues as before. The project is managed as a departmental activity hidden from any organizational visibility.

A common misconception

The idea for the project will almost certainly be created from your knowledge and experience of the organization, customer base or market place. This 'technical' knowledge is often considered as the perfect qualification for leading a project team to a successful

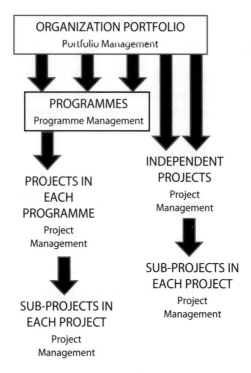

Figure 2.1   Relationships in portfolio Management

outcome. You are the 'technical expert' and any subsequent success or failure is attached to you. It is also commonly believed that as the expert you can manage the work of the project in the same way as normal day to day activities and will take the same amount of time. Assumptions are made creating false expectations of cost and time to complete that can rarely be satisfied in practice. The relationships are shown in Figure 2.1

WHAT'S THE CURRENT CLIMATE?

The projects are conducted within the prevailing climate in your organization. Perhaps this climate is:

- Stormy and riddled with conflict,
- Continually subject to reactive activities due to systems failures
- Subject to outside influences not identified as possible happenings
- Focused totally on today and never considering tomorrow

If this is the case, then much of the time the organization will strive to overcome the conditions that prevail in which everyone tries to get their job done to the best of their ability. People are left operating in a climate of many unknowns, trying to resolve conflicts with no analysis of the future, no risk analysis and no forecast of what problems will hit them tomorrow. Senior managers are continually reacting and fire-fighting, not looking ahead to business development. Project work comes to a halt as team members are continually re-assigned or overloaded with operational and fire-fighting activities. The climate for project work to succeed does not exist in such a culture.

It is essential for senior managers to create and work continually to sustain the climate for success. As project manager you are more likely to be remembered for your failures rather than your successes so you have a key role to play in supporting and maintaining the climate for success.

INFLUENCE OF ORGANIZATIONAL CULTURE

The prevailing culture of an organization is often quoted as the reason why things do not happen as planned or intended. The concept of culture is difficult to define or explain precisely and little consensus exists on its meaning or relationship with the climate in the organization.

A common and simple way of defining culture is 'how things get done round here'. It generally identifies what is 'acceptable and not acceptable' and what behaviours are encouraged and discouraged. Most attempts to open this definition to analysis focus on:

*the collection of traditions, values, policies, beliefs and
attitudes that constitute a pervasive context for everything
we do in an organization.*

So we can expect culture to be influenced by the system of rites, rituals, patterns of communication and expected behaviours that are acceptable. For example, a senior manager who says 'do not tell me about the risks in your project, that is negative thinking' is creating a belief and pattern of behaviour denying that any risk could possibly interfere with the integrity of your project. You are then expected to ensure you mitigate all risks, whether foreseen or unforeseen and avoid any issues ever occurring. This is avoiding the reality that creating change or something new, moving into the unknown is not a fully controlled process.

 KEY FACT

Management is the key influence on culture through their style of leadership and the staff acceptance of the climate created leading to the environment in which the organization operates with a quick response and adaptation to change when it is required.

WHAT INFLUENCES CULTURE

Behaviour is strongly influenced by the perceptions people have of the internal climate. Acceptance or otherwise of the existing culture has a significant impact on climate. The key elements in the climate that impact on your ability to achieve success with your project also include some less obvious cultural influences:

- Morale
- Mutual trust, support and respect for decisions
- Openness and integrity – avoiding confrontation
- Risk taking and optimism – recognition of risks and sharing in success
- Freedom of action – through accountability, pride and participation in decision making
- Commitment – a sense of belonging, avoiding confusion with clear responsibilities
- Collaboration – shared beliefs, teamwork and mutual assistance, minimizing stress
- Training – opportunities to learn both on and off the job

Paying specific attention to these influences is important for you. It is not enough to blame the management if the climate is going wrong. Perceptions of the climate are always stronger in the staff than among the management. This is not to suggest you are the standard-bearer for the whole organization, but you can work with your team to ensure each influence is given adequate attention.

INFLUENCE OF THE ORGANIZATION STRUCTURE

Many organizations are still structured formally into a hierarchy (Figure 2.2). This is easy to comprehend and manage creating a simple management structure that allows career progression, delegation of authority and clear demarcation of responsibilities based on skills and function. This type of structure has evolved as 'best practice' and supports a manufacturing or service-oriented organization where each function has a part to play that is well defined.

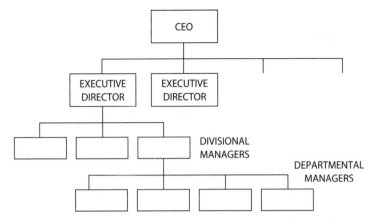

Figure 2.2 A hierarchical structure

Introduce the project into this structure and difficulties immediately appear. If a change activity or project is confined to one vertical leg or functional area the principal issues to resolve are resource availability and time management. As soon as a project team is required that demands from different functions then problems occur.

Communication channels, accountability, decision making and reporting systems are designed to be effective vertically in the structure but frequently meet serious barriers across the organization.

Projects can and do succeed in spite of the issues these difficulties create. The project leader must be very committed to break down the numerous cross-functional barriers but this does consume effort that could be better expended on the project work.

KEY FACT

A significant key to project success is effective collaborative working across the organization structure breaking down functional boundaries. This encourages the recognition that the assignment of an individual to a project team for a specific part of available time is a dedicated assignment for the whole project.

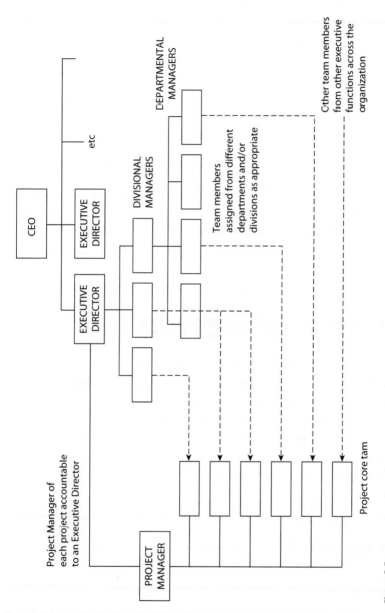

Figure 2.3 A project-based matrix structure

This collaborative working creates a weak matrix structure for projects but has some formality and acceptance by the management, the resulting cross-functional team has the benefit of effective utilization of the total available resources between the functional operational work and the projects the organization needs to complete. The projects initiated in the organization create a virtual structure alongside the hierarchy that holds all the resources. Dedicated resources are clearly identified with their temporary re-assignment (see Figure 2.3).

This structure introduces the need for new specifically designed systems of performance management taking where a functional manager must take performance data from a project manager when conducting appraisals. Financial controls have to take into account the divided responsibilities for any team member but this is not beyond the capabilities of financial control systems and is also included in most project management software systems.

INFLUENCE OF THE BUSINESS STRATEGY

It is important to clearly understand why any project is initiated and establish a defined process to focus on the reasons and purpose. The link here is the business strategy of the organization.

Although the vision of the senior management team is not always obvious or clearly stated, there is always a fundamental direction that the business is striving to sustain. This drives the strategy that normally can be simplified down to three elements:

- Sustaining existing activities for incremental growth and benefit creation
- Maintaining a focus on initiated projects to gain additional benefits
- Identifying new projects that will provide further additional benefits

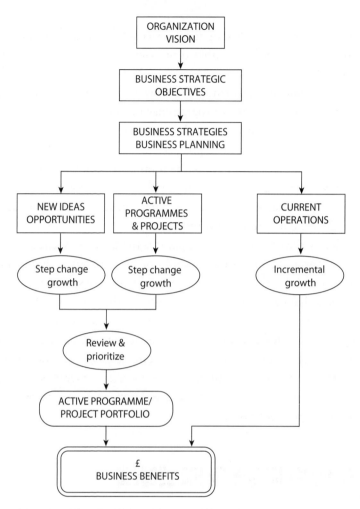

Figure 2.4 How strategy and projects are related

KEY FACT

If projects are undertaken that do not align with the business strategy then there is a risk that valuable resources and funds are being used to create something the business does not need or cannot use.

There is also a hidden lost opportunity cost because those resources and funds are not being utilized on something the business does need.

Programme management is the basis of managing the complete portfolio. The concept of programmes in this context is a collection of related projects that work together to provide benefits over a period of time. This does not preclude the use of independent projects that also form part of the total portfolio. Generally Programme Management is concerned with overall strategic objectives and is very suited to enabling the management of the impact and benefits from a number of projects.

Clearly the essential starting point is the business strategy. Any new programme or project should not be initiated without first testing that it fits the existing strategy or justifies, in special circumstances, a change to the strategy. Always ask the question: 'Why are we attempting to do this?' It is remarkable how managers will justify the strategic fit by clever use of semantics, particularly as strategies are frequently fairly broad statements in their own right. Strategic fit alone does not guarantee success, it merely serves to ensure we are doing the right thing and not doing something that has no alignment to business needs.

THE OPERATING CLIMATE FOR SUCCESS

Although culture, formal structure, and business strategy provide important contributions towards the prevailing climate, the cement that holds everything together is the operating infrastructure. This is what enables good decisions to be made and ensure that focus for all the activities and projects are directed towards satisfying the needs and objectives of the business strategy. Creating this infrastructure ensures that all the key players in the organization project environment have clearly defined roles and responsibilities. A balanced, holistic view of the business must be taken to ensure all the resources available are effectively utilized to grow

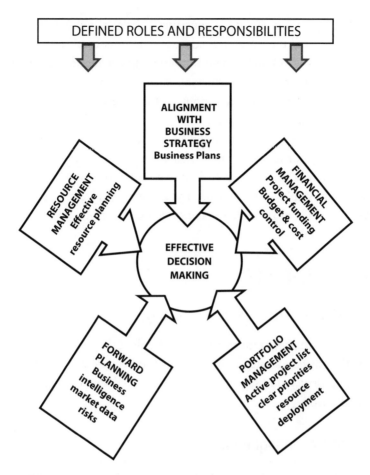

Figure 2.5 The project climate for success – key activities

and develop the business. This transcends the more parochial view often supported by the hierarchical structure. Decisions can only be effective if they are based on real and accurate information. This creates the need for supporting systems to collect data to enable management to make informed decisions rather than rely on inspired guesswork. The selection and continuation of all project activities is costly, consuming resources, and must be based on informed decisions.

The operating climate is constructed from many contributing activities from the culture, organizational infrastructure and strategy, but we can collect these into some key activities that make a significant impact to achieving success with all the projects. All these activities provide input to the core activity – effective decision processing (Figure 2.5).

Decisions on projects should be made by senior management based on informed judgement that is trusted, respected and supported across the organization. It is essential to avoid conflicting decisions, duplication of effort and allowing projects that should be suspended or cancelled to continue like 'runaway trains'.

THE KEY ACTIVITIES

Alignment with business strategy

Projects and programmes are selected only if they support achieving the business strategy and contribute to business growth. A carefully constructed Business case is an essential document supporting the decision.

Resource management

Resource needs of existing commitments must be visible and known and the available capacity to take on more work in new projects needs to be clear to everyone. If resource planning is not practised you do not know if you have sufficient resource capacity to complete what has already started let alone start new projects.

Financial management

Adequate funding must be available to satisfy the budget of all active projects. If you do not know what it will cost, the business cannot adequately plan cash flow and make provision for future project needs, which may lead to suspended or cancelled projects.

Portfolio management

Maintaining a visible, authorized list of active projects and those waiting to start is essential to inform everyone of priorities and relative importance of those on the list. Without this listing interdependencies are not clear and the authorized projects are not visible to the whole organization. Timescale and completion targets need to be agreed to meet the business and/or customer needs and plan the effective deployment of resources.

Forward planning

The selection of projects requires the organization to plan ahead using adequate intelligence gathered from the market place and customers. This avoids biased decisions, lack of focus on critical areas of potential business growth and lost opportunities.

THE KEY PLAYERS – DEFINED ROLES AND RESPONSIBILITIES

For your project to achieve a successful outcome you need to identify the principal roles of all the key players in the business and their responsibilities both for operating and project activities and how they will work together – the infrastructure. This avoids confusion and clarifies where authority exists to make decisions and avoid unnecessary slippage and delays in projects.

For every project, apart from the originator of the idea or opportunity we need:

- Someone who need the benefits – the company senior management

- Someone who wants to use, influence or is affected by the outcomes – the customer, the stakeholders
- Someone who is accountable for achieving the benefits – the sponsor
- Someone who is accountable for the project work – the project manager
- Someone who is responsible for the project work – the project team
- Someone who commits to provide the resources – line managers

Together this whole group creates an infrastructure that is over-laid on the functional hierarchy, and their behaviour collectively can determine the degree of success that is achievable with all the projects. The relationships are shown in Figure 2.6.

KEY FACT

The relationships in a project environment can only lead to success when there is a clear definition of ownership at each level in the organization with clearly defined roles and responsibilities.

A new term has appeared in this chapter – the *stakeholders*. These are the people who have a specific and clearly definable interest in your project – a stake in gambling terms! We cannot ignore anyone who wants to use, influence or is affected by the out-comes – these are the customer(s) and the stakeholders. They are an important group of people and Chapter 6 is devoted to the management of this group.

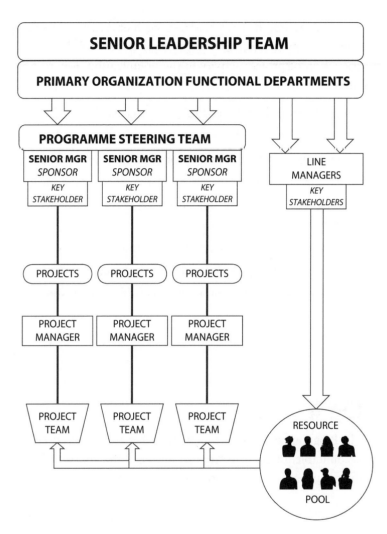

Figure 2.6 Infrastructure for projects

Programme Steering Team [PST]

This group made up of senior managers, meets at regular intervals to review the status of all active projects. The PST is essential, particularly for projects that cross functional boundaries, to ensure decisions are made collaboratively, carried out effectively and the Sponsors accept their role and responsibilities. The PST selects and initiates new projects, resolves major issues and decides the prioritization of project activity in the organization. Key responsibilities include:

- management of the total portfolio of projects
- ensuring projects are aligned to business strategy and objectives
- giving strategic direction taking forward plans into account
- maintaining focus on customer and balancing business needs
- ensuring environmental influences are taken into account (internal and external)
- prioritizing all active projects and their resource needs
- resolving escalated issues related to cross-functional working
- ultimate decision forum for all major problems and issues
- approves start-up, suspension and cancellation decisions on projects

KEY FACT

The Programme Steering Team is the owner and is collectively accountable for the effective management and control of the organization's Portfolio of programmes and projects.

The portfolio cannot be owned by one individual – not even the chief executive! The members of the PST are the *Project Sponsors*, some taking responsibility for just one project or programme and some taking responsibility for several. If teamwork at senior levels in the organization is poor, the PST is ineffective because it appears to have a low added value to the active programmes and projects. This is frequently because the Sponsors do not openly accept or understand their role or responsibilities.

Project sponsor

The *Project sponsor* for any project is accountable (to the PST) for the overall performance of their project(s) to provide the organization with the benefits promised in the approved business case. The sponsor must openly commit to the role and demonstrate a concern for success. Key responsibilities include:

- ensuring project objectives are always aligned to business needs
- selecting the Project Manager
- approving the project definition and sustaining the project direction
- ensuring priorities are maintained for all their projects
- reacting promptly with decisions on escalated issues
- demonstrating support to the project manager and team

KEY FACT

The Sponsor is exclusively accountable for oversight management and control of the project process, procedures, approving performance to targets and budget. There can only be one sponsor for each project.

Do not confuse with a line management role; the sponsor does not own all the resources, but must commit to giving adequate time to these responsibilities.

The Project Manager

The Project Manager is responsible for the day to day management of the project work from the initial kick-off through to closure. Key responsibilities include:

- selecting the core team with the *Project Sponsor*
- identifying and managing the project stakeholders
- defining the project and securing stakeholder approval
- planning the project and securing stakeholder approval
- identifying and managing the risks
- controlling changes and updating the business case
- securing resource commitments and allocating resources to the work
- monitoring and tracking project progress
- solving the problems that interfere with progress
- controlling costs
- leading the project team
- informing stakeholders of progress status
- delivering the project deliverables and benefits
- managing performance of everyone involved with the project

KEY FACT

The Project Manager is accountable to the Sponsor for managing the performance of everyone involved with the project to deliver the objectives and benefits.

The project team

There are three types of project team:

- Functional team
- Cross-functional team
- Inter-company team

Functional teams are confined to one department in the organization, so the department manager takes the role of Sponsor for all the department projects, appointing members of the department to the roles of Project Manager and Team member. This is generally confined to smaller projects that do not require input or assistance of other departments in the project work.

Larger projects and all programmes will either involve cross-functional or inter-company teams.

Cross-functional teams composed of people from different functions within one organization are common. This can lead to a new culture with a broader view that says, 'We're all in this together'. Success is team success and rewards are team rewards. If the project fails the team members share the blame. The essence of a team is common commitment. Without it, groups perform as individuals but with it, they become a powerful unit of collective performance. The cross-functional team has specific advantages that allow organizations to:

- Reduce the time for product development
- Improve ability to solve complex problems
- Focus resources on satisfying customer needs
- Develop new technical and professional skills
- Promote more effective intra- and inter-teamwork

To accrue these benefits each member of a cross-functional team must focus on three essential elements to be effective:

- Being an effective team player
- Being an effective team
- Building effective inter-team relationships

Inter-company teams have the same issues as cross-functional teams but on a larger scale and for very large projects will involve several organizations. This requires careful consideration of the responsibilities of the key players – the programme and project sponsors and the project managers for each project in each organization involved. Effective communication is an essential ingredient of success in any project environment but particularly when several organizations are involved which may be in widely dispersed locations from different cultures.

The project team member

The team members are responsible for the timely completion of all the work set out in the plan and schedule. Any individual team member may be accountable for a package of the work when delegated authority by the Project Manager, eg as Leader of a sub-project team.

There are two types of team member:

- the core team member – who remains part of the team right through the project and is often or preferably, dedicated to the role full time or for a significant part of their capacity (ie > 60 per cent).

- the extended team member – who joins the team for a limited period of time just when their skills and knowledge are needed and may have no further involvement later in the project. Extended team members usually but not always work under the close direction of a core team member.

Responsibilities of the core team member include:

- accept and commit to the team role
- liaise and work with other team members to get their work done
- contribute to the project documentation
- participate in planning and risk management
- monitor and manage progress of their assigned work packages
- resolve issues or escalate them to the project manager
- participate in problem solving

- identify potential risks, issues, opportunities
- support and assist other team members when appropriate

Similar responsibilities exist for the extended team members and it is important for you to ensure that all team members accept these responsibilities from the outset.

KEY FACT

All team members must know to whom they report and what is expected of them. In large complex projects this is often a source of confusion.

It helps to create an organization chart for the project and clearly define any authority you delegate to a core team member.

Being an effective team player

A team is a collection of individuals and what each brings to the team can make the difference between success or failure. Each team member is selected to contribute specific skills, knowledge and experience essential to achieving the project objectives. When each team player lives up to their potential then the team has a high probability of success. When one or more of the team players do not fulfill their obligations and responsibilities then the team's chances of success are severely damaged. Success requires that the team players give maximum contributions and this demands that senior management ensures they are given:

- Additional skills required, encouragement and support
- The environment to identify individual strengths and weaknesses
- Opportunities to develop plans to increase their effectiveness.

Becoming an effective team in a project environment

When a group of individuals come together, something happens regardless of their previous relationships. The interaction, dynamics and leadership all combine to create a sum greater than the individual parts. Use the checklist to determine your team effectiveness. If you cannot answer 'yes' to each question then examine what actions are necessary to improve your team performance.

CHECKLIST NO 1 – TEAM EFFECTIVENESS

- Does the leader have the necessary team management skills? ☐
- Is the authority clear and consistent with the team's responsibilities? ☐
- Does the team have and understand the project objectives? ☐
- Do the team members participate in key team decisions? ☐
- Are the team members clear about their role and responsibilities? ☐
- Does the team give high priority to developing relationships with project key stakeholders? ☐
- Are team meetings well planned and executed? ☐
- Does Management actively support the team? ☐
- Are customer representatives included in the team? ☐
- Are differences and conflict resolved openly in the team? ☐
- Is the team's primary focus on satisfying key stakeholders and customer needs? ☐

With the answers to these questions the team can then work to:

- Identify the team strengths and develop plans ☐
  to build on them.
- Develop improvement opportunities and ☐
  then derive action plans to implement.

A cross-functional team does not operate in isolation but in a collection of other teams and key stakeholders in the organization. Boundary management of stakeholders is a critical key element for success. The team must develop strong relationships with senior management, functional department managers, key support groups, customer(s) and suppliers to ensure they have effective collaboration. It cannot be assumed that others in the organization are interested or care about their work and in practice may even work against them.

Obstacles to team success

Project success is totally dependent on team effectiveness and inevitably barriers will emerge. Use the checklist on pp 40–42 to eliminate many of the common obstacles.

CHECKLIST NO 2 – OBSTACLES TO TEAM EFFECTIVENESS

Limitations of Team Leadership

Does the Leader:

- Have the technical knowledge to understand the 'big picture'? ☐
- Really understand the potential contributions of the team members? ☐
- Have the skills to manage the team members who have had little experience working together? ☐
- Have proven ability to manage meetings effectively, resolve conflicts and communicate well? ☐
- Involve everyone in team decisions? ☐
- Fully utilize team members' skills? ☐

Uncertain team authority

- Does the team have the authority to make and take decisions and then implement them? ☐
- Does the team engage with key stakeholders? ☐
- Does the team feel empowered, demonstrate strong commitment, clear focus and a desire to succeed? ☐

Ambiguous or unclear objectives and goals

Does the team have:

- A clear vision or understanding of what is expected of them? ☐
- Individual work plans clearly identified? ☐

- A clear understanding how their work fits in the big picture? □
- Team goals established and agreed by the whole team collectively to ensure understanding, acceptance, and commitment? □
- Clear team goals which synchronize with individual goals and performance objectives? □
- Regular reviews of objectives and goals as changes occur? □

Managing the boundaries

Has the team:

- Identified the key stakeholders? □
- Created a Stakeholder list and assigned responsibilities? (see Chapter 6) □
- Ensured the Project Sponsor is engaged with the project work at all stages? □

Performance

Do the team members:

- Know their activities and work in the project team will be evaluated in performance reviews? □
- Feel recognized as part of the team even when they are transient members for a short time? □
- Have regular performance discussions with both the Project Manager and their Functional Manager? (if different) □
- Know the Project Manager communicates performance information back to their respective Functional Manager □

Team dynamics

Does the Project Manager:

- Work to ensure there is no conflict in the team? ☐

- Take action promptly when conflict arises? ☐

- Take time to understand the work style, practices and other baggage of the team members? ☐

- Try to introduce some elements of training in team dynamics where time allows? ☐

- Openly encourage discussion of professional, technical and personal differences and opinions? ☐

- Strive to achieve a resolution of differences? ☐

- Maintain an 'open door' policy? ☐

- Demonstrate a concern to maintain good working relationships in the team? ☐

No team can achieve without management support and especially the cross-functional team which is highly dependent on active senior management and functional management support from these key stakeholders in the PST.

KEY FACT

One of the greatest obstacles to success is the failure of the key stakeholders to:

- work with, co-operate and support the team or
- alternatively actively sabotage the project team's efforts.

Creating successful cross-functional teams

It is fundamental to creating a successful business strategy that senior managers acknowledge the critical role of effective cross-functional teams. It is not enough to group people together, call them a team, provide some quick training and then expect rapid results. The senior management must be seen to act and behave as a successful cross-functional team and then provide and encourage active support at all levels of the organization. They must ensure the performance appraisal process and that the rewards and recognition system relate to business vision and objectives and recognize that the cross-functional team is a critical vehicle to implement the business strategy.

KEY FACT

A successful team-based organization is one where senior management is fully committed to eliminate inter-team barriers and competition for resources, and to avoid individual recognition, providing a performance measurement system that promotes interdependent achievement with individual accountability.

You must create the appropriate climate to enable you and your team to achieve success in your project. It is perhaps valid to note that all these influences are also considered as key to effective leadership, which indicates how closely climate and leadership are related.

SUMMARY

Ensure you

- Understand the difference between portfolio, programmes and projects.

- Explore what influences the operating climate in your organization.

- Identify the key roles and ensure the responsibilities for each are clearly understood.

- Understand what you can do to make your project team effective and successful.

THE PROJECT PROCESS –
KEY STEPS FOR SUCCESS

One of the key elements of success is the sharing of information particularly when the project work extends across different sites and countries. Ideally this should extend also to using common computer software for data recording and scheduling. The combined result is the creation of a common, shared 'language' in the team that saves much time with the improved communication this brings.

KEY FACT

It is essential that everyone involved agrees to use the same processes, procedures and standard documentation formats.

THE PROJECT PHASES

The project management process is well established and comprises six clearly definable phases with decision gates between each:

- project conception;
- project definition;
- project planning;
- project launch and execution;
- project closure;
- post-project evaluation.

Using this approach ensures all projects follow the same rational process and it is easy to review and report progress for each relative to the others. These phases are intentionally sequential and in each phase you will carry out specific activities that generate the data for decision processing. These activities are often referred to as 'key stages' as they may comprise several actual tasks carried out by more than one person.

Although each phase is treated as discrete with specific work to be completed, this does not signify they are 'one-off' activities. In reality the phases are often revisited during a project. Once a project is initiated, the need to reiterate some or all of the work done in the definition or planning phases is always a possibility as the project moves ahead in the execution phase.

In practice these phases are only a convenience for you to separate the project work into blocks with a defined sequence. The reality is that no project follows such a neat and simple process flow without a significant amount of reiteration. At any stage of the project work you may have to:

- revise the project definition;
- re-plan part of the work;

- revise the project schedule;
- solve problems;
- carry out recovery planning – to recover lost time;
- carry out contingency planning – in case a high risk part of the work goes wrong.

Completion of any phase in the process requires a decision-making process to be invoked. The work done must be subjected to a rigorous review to determine the validity of allowing the programme or project to continue. This decision can commit the organization to resources that do not exist due to other commitments, so a careful analysis of resource utilization must be made by the management to help make this decision. Too often rogue programmes or projects are allowed to continue unchecked and either subsequently fail due to insufficient resources or seriously impact other important programmes by stealing their resources. Clearly the technical feasibility of continuing must be reviewed at the same time. In the past many development projects (eg for a new product) have become 'runaway trains' consuming huge amounts of resources and still subsequently failing with large debt write-offs. Such situations can be reduced or avoided using a rigorous regular review and decision process.

THE PHASE GATES

This decision process can only work effectively with the two major components:

1 *Phase Gates* – at various stages of the project a phase gate is located between the phases and this provides entry to the next phase of the project or programme process.

A Phase Gate can only be opened by the decision of the PST, sometimes conditional if the work of the previous phase is incomplete, yet some work in the next phase can proceed.

2 *The Programme Steering Team (PST).* This team of senior managers who are also the project and programme sponsors meet at regular intervals to review the reported status of all active programmes and projects. The PST also approves opportunities to be investigated and sets the priorities.

The Programme Steering Team is the ultimate decision making group for all projects and programmes, their progress, delay, suspension or cancellation. The PST is acting in the best interests of the organization so their decisions are final and cannot be countered by any individual.

The phase gate serves to allow the PST to:

- validate the project is still needed;
- confirm the project risks are still acceptable;
- confirm the priority relative to other projects;
- accept any validation or revision of the business case;
- make a 'GO/NO GO' decision about continuing.

Then three essential questions have to be asked as shown in Figure 3.1.

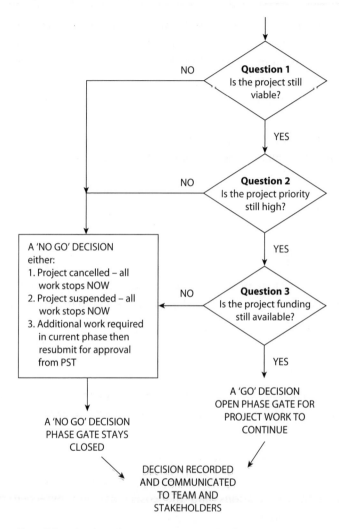

Figure 3.1 The three key questions at each phase gate

THE PHASE GATE – A CONSTRAINT?

Does the concept of the gate at the end of the phase constitute a constraint by preventing some work in the next phase starting in the interests of saving time? The purpose of the gate is to focus everyone in taking a deep breath and just asking 'where are we now?' Only the PST can open the gate to grant entry to the next phase. The PST can make this decision under specific circumstances even if the work of the previous phase is incomplete. The PST will expect to be given some clear plan to complete the work of an active phase when opening the gate to the next phase in this way.

KEY FACT

The phase gate must never be viewed as a constraint on the work of the project, but the gates are mandatory for all projects.

After a detailed review of the status of a project at the end of a phase, the PST is primarily concerned to seek answers to three questions:

- Is the programme or project still viable?
  The PST must be satisfied that the planned benefits meet its original expectations and the costs have not exceeded the planned budget.

- Is the priority the same relative to other programmes or projects?
  The PST decides the relative priority of all active programmes and projects taking into account the costs, benefits and resource availability.

- Is funding still available?

  The PST must decide to continue funding the work when reviewing all other commitments. In some circumstances the work may be slowed to make money available for other activities.

After a successful review and with satisfactory answers to the above questions the next phase gate is opened and a 'GO' decision recorded. However the PST may decide one of three primary options:

- **Terminate** – cancel the programme or project and initiate decommissioning procedures immediately to minimize collateral damage.

- **Suspend work** – stop all work temporarily for a specified period. This may be due to a change of priority, moving resources to another programme, financial constraints or a demand for a review of strategic needs.

- **Reiterate** – go back and repeat past work or additional work in the current phase with revisions to the definition, scope or plans.

Any of these options will lead to a 'NO GO' decision being recorded. If the decision is 'Reiterate' then you will be expected to take appropriate action on the reasons for the decision and then present your programme or project again for review at an agreed future meeting of the PST.

Under certain circumstances the PST may require more work to be done in a phase before opening the gate, requesting a reiteration of some activities in more detail perhaps. Alternatively a decision may be made to suspend all work at the time to allow a more important project to take precedence.

THE KEY STEPS TO SUCCESS

Each of the phases in a project is a key step towards a successful outcome. They are interdependent and all closely linked together in a logical manner. Two key processes, stakeholder management and risk and issue management, have a significant impact on your success.

The business case is generated in the initial phase to enable a decision to proceed. This should remain a living document, subject to review and validation at each phase gate. If the project direction is proceeding contrary to the contents of the business case then a conscious decision must be made to continue with the project. The business case may require amendment itself, as new information becomes available. The impact of any changes to the business case must be assessed as part of the review and validation process.

You have to consider two other activities that impact on the project success, each having a continuous effect on the project performance. Risks are inherent in all projects and the management of risk is so important to your success it demands constant attention throughout the project. The effort may typically vary in each phase but risk management cannot be avoided if you seek to achieve a successful outcome. Similarly the management of your stakeholders is equally important. The stakeholders are often powerful sources of influence, and failure to manage them effectively can lead to disaster.

Each of the key steps, the phases of the project process, managing stakeholders and managing risk will be examined in more detail in the following chapters.

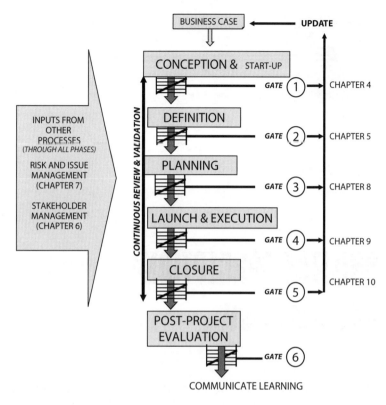

Figure 3.2   The project phases and gates

SUMMARY

Ensure your team understand:

- The six project phases and the principles of the phase gates
- How the phase gates are used for decision processing
- The key steps to success in project work

PROJECT CONCEPTION AND START-UP

Most projects start from an initial idea, either from a potential customer or generated inside the organization. Such ideas usually abound, far exceeding the available resources or funding for them all to be realistically turned into active projects. An initial screening process is essential if the organization is not to over-commit resources and fail to deliver the desired results. This may involve some simple form of written proposal or just be a management decision to derive the initial business case. As a general rule it is preferable to derive the initial business case as a basis for informed decisions to be made.

SELECTING THE RIGHT PROJECT

The decision to initiate a project is usually taken by the senior management through the PST who need to be given enough data by you to make that decision. Selecting the wrong new project may impact existing active projects and precipitate failure.

There are two fundamental approaches to the selection process:

- A model generating quantitative data
- A model generating only qualitative data

KEY FACT

Any proposed project or business case must by definition align with the declared business strategy for the PST to give the proposal any consideration.

If the climate is appropriate then a strategic fit is a prerequisite for the PST to even consider a project proposal or business case. Every organization should develop its own way of conducting this process to ensure the total portfolio of active projects does not demand more funds or resources than can be provided to achieve success.

Figure 4.1 illustrates one approach where the PST based on an initial business case or proposal conducts the initial screening of ideas and opportunities for projects. Those approved for more detailed scrutiny are then subject to a full needs and expectations analysis by an initial core team along with a review of resource needs. This data is used to generate a full business case for the proposed project. A secondary screening by the PST reviews the full business case before opening the gate to the definition phase. At each screening some opportunities are dropped completely or confined to a 'wait bin' for later consideration.

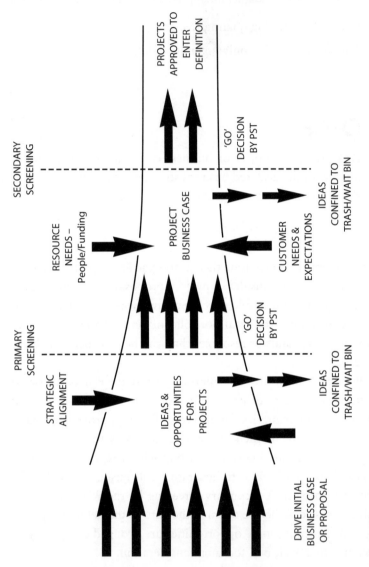

Figure 4.1 Selecting the right projects

Any project selection process requires the PST to ask some basic questions:

- Will the proposed project maximize profits?
- Will the proposed project:
  - maintain market share?
  - consolidate market position?
  - open up new markets?
- Will the project maximize utilization of existing resources (ie people)?
- Will the project maximize the utilization of existing manufacturing capacity?
- Will the project boost company image?
- Will the project increase risk faced by the company?
- Is the project scope within the company's current skills and experience?

The model can be constructed more rigorously by weighting some factors as more important than others indicating their value in contributing to the company objectives at the time. A detailed list of factors can be developed as appropriate based on:

- technology;
- marketing;
- finance;
- manufacture;
- personnel;
- administration.

This can lead to a long list of factors, which is an advantage of this approach, and if these factors are then weighted a complex model can be derived that provides a score at the end. Such a model can readily be automated as a web-based tool making it easy to apply sensitivity analysis to any of the factors.

This method does have some disadvantages. All listed items:

- appear to have equal importance if not weighted;
- have a different degree of risk and uncertainty;
- have a different degree of complexity.

In addition the list may include unknown errors, redundant items or some that are difficult to quantify owing to lack of data. However, this approach does have the benefit of encouraging you to ask a lot of questions to validate the selection of the project and help the PST make an informed decision.

KEY FACT

The diversity of opinion within the PST leads to more effective decision processing and avoids emotive, often poorly informed project decisions by one individual.

QUANTITATIVE MODELS

Most quantitative models will focus on financial data to support the case. The data generated varies widely but may include information on:

- return on investment;
- return on net assets;
- breakeven and payback period;
- cost of risks;
- net present value and/or internal rate of return;
- cost–benefit analysis;
- sensitivity analysis;
- market data.

Each of the financial techniques has its merits and disadvantages so it is common to use more than one of the above. The more data generated, the more effort required later to re-validate and measure actual performance when all the focus is on the project work.

Another approach is to derive a formula based on certain key information to compare project opportunities, eg for projects creating new products or services:

PROJECT INDEX = ([F × P] × n × d) / 100 × C

Where:

F = forecast sales volume

P = forecast net profit on sales

n = probability of technical success

d = time discount factor

C = forecast total cost of the project to completion

The time discount factor is a weighting based on forecasts of achieving a successful outcome on time to meet the sales forecasts from 1 (on time) to 0 (never completed). The method is not rigorous but provided common units are used it can be a useful additional tool that can readily be adapted to suit many types of business. Of course like many of these approaches it does require team judgement to be exercised.

Many organizations depend on investment and net asset returns calculations to make decisions. For project work it is suggested that cost–benefit analysis should also be used as a matter of good practice. However a cost–benefit analysis does not give the feeling of absolute size and benefits of the compared projects unless some weighting system is introduced to take account of relative size, costs or time to complete. A simple way of ranking projects based on benefits can be carried out using a simple matrix as shown in Figure 4.2.

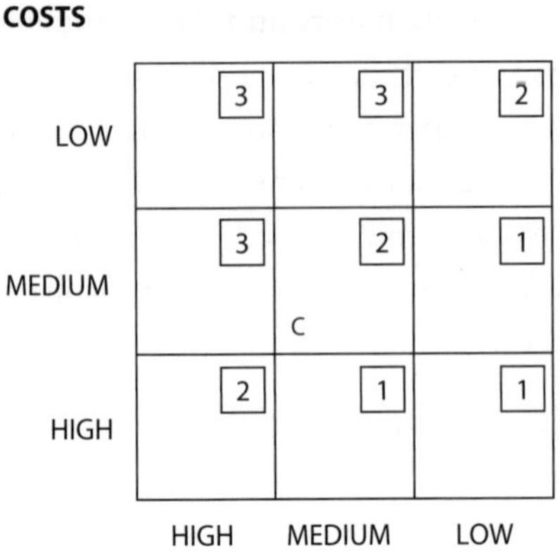

COSTS

	HIGH	MEDIUM	LOW
LOW	3	3	2
MEDIUM	3	2	1
		C	
HIGH	2	1	1

Note: The number in each box of the matrix is the score assigned to each project that falls in that box. To compare all potential projects sum the scores achieved in each benefit matrix used for analysis. See the table below.

The highest score is potentially the most likely project to succeed with maximum benefits for the business.

BENEFIT

Financial, Technical, Operational, Marketing, Business Fit

PROJECT SELECTION – BENEFIT ANALYSIS							
PROJECTS		SOURCE FROM BENEFIT MATRIX					
No	Title	Financial	Technical	Operational	Marketing	Business Fit	TOTAL
A		3	2	2	1	2	10
B		2	3	2	3	2	12
C		1	2	3	1	1	8
D		3	3	2	3	2	13
E		2	2	3	1	2	10
F		3	3	3	2	3	14
G		3	2	2	1	2	10

PROJECT 'F' SHOULD BE SELECTED BUT PROJECTS 'B' AND 'D' SHOULD BE REVIEWED BEFORE A FINAL DECISION IS MADE

Figure 4.2 Cost–benefit matrix

Create a separate matrix for each of the following benefits and add others as required:

- Financial
- Technical
- Operational

- Marketing
- Fit with business strategy

Alternatively this method is readily adapted and enhanced as a spreadsheet calculation to rank all the potential projects and derive an 'Overall Ranking Score' for each to show which have the lowest cost and highest benefits.

All these and other methods are only a means of generating a guide based on available data, much of which is potentially suspect anyway because it is based on forecasts and estimates with sometimes huge unknowns still present. The more techniques that are used the better the PST is equipped in the decision process. Frequently the business case will contain both qualitative and quantitative data for decision processing.

KEY FACT

The key controlling document, the Business Case is the fundamental charter for the project and must be subject to regular revisits, review, updating and re-approval by the PST.

As more information becomes available through the project, complete and enhance the data in the business case. Do pay attention to your configuration management and record all revisions or additions made. It is important that the PST always refers to the latest revision when revisiting its decisions.

Use the checklist as a guide to the inputs required for project selection.

CHECKLIST NO 3 – INPUTS TO PROJECT SELECTION

- *The potential profit growth*
  - Return on investment
  - Return on nets assets
  - Breakeven and payback period
  - Cost of risks
  - Net present value and/or Internal rate of return
  - Benefit/Cost ratio
  - Sensitivity analysis

- *Change to market share*
  - Maintain current market position
  - Consolidate market position
  - Open up new markets

- *Changes to risk level*
  - Technical risks
  - Scheduling risks
  - Organizational disruption
  - Impact on current customer base
  - Risk of not doing the programme or project
  - Why do it now?

- *Maximize the utilization of current manufacturing capacity*

- *Need for new manufacturing capacity*

- *Maximize the utilization of existing resources (ie people)*

- *Need additional people and/or skills*

- *Improvement of Organization's public image and reputation*

- *Improvements to the Organization internal culture*

  - Eliminates or improves existing business processes
  - Changes to job satisfaction
  - Reduction of administration burden

THE START-UP PROCESS

You are enthusiastic and keen to dive in and get going and show some activity. It is prudent to review just what information you can now assemble to ensure the project does not set off in the wrong direction. At this stage you should have clarified:

- who your sponsor is;
- who the customer and possible secondary customers are;
- who will use the results;
- the initial project core team – or likely candidates;
- other people who can influence the project – the stakeholders.

Your efforts and the work of the team will now be focused on gathering information from this group of individuals to kick-off the project (see Figure 4.3).

CUSTOMER NEEDS AND EXPECTATIONS

Defining the needs of the customer starts off a process that will ultimately allow you to produce deliverables specifically designed to meet the customer's expectations. Once you have established a clear understanding of the needs you can develop the requirements that drive the planning process.

Working with your customers can be frustrating. At times you will need to exercise all your communication skills to achieve a good, open relationship enabling the project to move ahead to achieve the agreed objectives. Deriving the needs statement is a product of a partnership between you and your customer. This places an obligation on your customer to enter into the partnership with a serious intent to contribute openly and not sit on hidden agendas.

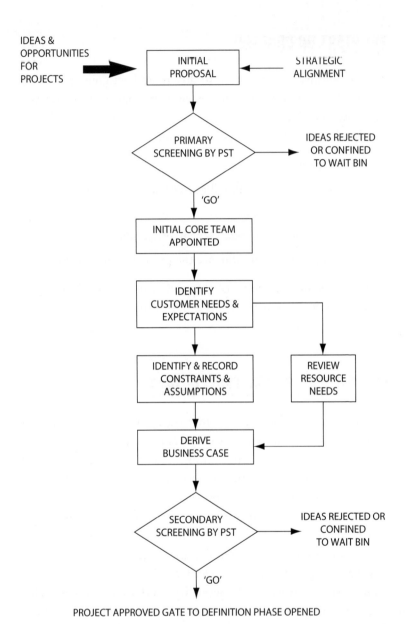

Figure 4.3 The start-up process

KEY FACT

Your business case will be permanently flawed if you do not understand the needs and expectations of your customer.

Exploring the needs of the customer will ultimately allow you to produce the list of deliverables specifically designed to meet the customer's expectations. Once you have established a clear understanding of the needs and validated these with the customer you can develop the requirements that drive the planning process.

You can develop a superbly detailed plan but it never compensates for misunderstood needs or poorly specified requirements to satisfy those needs. Needs are the minimum requirements to satisfy the customer. There are always additional expectations on the customer's 'wish list' that will hopefully also be satisfied. These may be exposed but are frequently hidden from you initially until they suddenly appear later as the dreaded 'scope creep' that so often upsets many project plans.

Some customers will suddenly find new needs out of new possibilities that only become apparent as the work proceeds. Frequently customers are expressive about what they do not need without really understanding what they do need!

You must make a particular effort and give adequate time to:

- understand the customer – explore priority and relative importance to other activities;
- understand the customer's environment in which they must operate;
- help the customer understand real 'needs' and avoid 'wishes'
- use political skills – not all customers are equal and some needs cannot be addressed;

- demonstrate your technical competence and awareness of their technical needs;
- convert ill-defined needs into practical solutions;
- keep an open mind and a creative approach;
- analyze the mixed signals you receive through personal influences on needs;
- attempt to expose the hidden expectations.

Your purpose at this stage is to turn the information you receive into a clear *statement of need* that you can reflect back to the customer for validation and acceptance with no ambiguity. Then both you and the customer are ready to collaborate fully to drive the project to a successful conclusion.

Avoid these potential traps:

1 Do not offer gold when silver is adequate – avoid striving for technical perfection beyond current capability or known state of the art. Confirm that the customer understands the risks of going for leading edge solutions.

2 Effect of bias filters – it is easy for you to ignore needs for which you cannot think of an easy solution because it is outside your experience or knowledge.

3 Dynamic needs – today's needs are not necessarily the same as next week's, next month's or next year's. Explore medium- to long-term needs as well.

4 Need ignorance – do any customers have a lack of knowledge (or a short term view only) that limits their understanding of what they really need medium to long term?

5 Mixing the needs of multiple customers. Take particular care to avoid the 'lower level', but still important needs for some customers, to get lost in a 'black hole' while you focus on the high level needs. Convenient simplification of need is a potential risk for the project and will inevitably lead to issues later.

6 Selective filtration – avoid filtering out needs that are not apparently interesting, technically challenging or potentially not very profitable. Customer satisfaction is your goal.

7 'I know what you need' approach – DON'T tell any customer you know better than they do. Use your communication skills effectively to build their understanding of needs.

Do remember that most customers always know what they don't need after they have seen it, and any customer who says they know exactly what they need is probably wrong.

THE CUSTOMER 'CONTRACT'

As project manager you have an obligation to turn your relationship with the customer into a form of contract. Often this is not a formal document signed by all parties but is an informal understanding. It is appropriate to document some form of agreement on the obligations of yourself and the customer, focused on achieving the agreed outcomes. This will lead you to define the roles and responsibilities of both parties to the contract, to carry out the project work.

Success is only possible if everyone involved fulfils their responsibilities and the customer cannot claim it as their right to act in complete independence. You must meet the customer requirements with constant attention to the triple constraints of project work – scope, cost and schedule. This is only possible if the customer acts promptly when necessary in resolving issues and giving approvals. Delays and cost overruns occur too easily if customer response is slow, suggesting the customer is not committed to a timely completion.

KEY FACT

Success is very dependent on your Customer understanding and accepting the project process you will use and integrate this with the way they work: this will avoid many potential roadblocks.

Use a checklist of questions to ask your customer(s) when you start to build the business case for the project:

CHECKLIST NO 4 – QUESTIONS FOR THE CUSTOMER

- What changes are identified?
  - Process changes?
  - Behaviour changes?
- Are these just a 'quick fix' or a quantum leap?
- What does the customer believe is needed?
- Do all customers agree?
- Have the fundamental needs been separated from wishes?
- Are pre-determined solutions being proposed already?
- Has the end user's perception of needs been identified?
- Have the needs been listed as primary, secondary and hopes?
- Has this list been prioritized and agreed with the customer?
- Can you turn the information into clear *'statements of need'*?
- Can you use the needs analysis to derive a *Statement of Requirements*?
- Will the *Customer* agree with your *Statement of Requirements*?

Build the checklist from project to project by adding additional questions to this list.

You will need much of this data when you get to the next key step of defining the project.

CUSTOMER SATISFACTION

Recognize that customer expectations directly relate to customer satisfaction. Unfortunately there are degrees of satisfaction relating to the extent to which your customer perceives you understand their expectations and, what is more important, meet them with the results achieved. Your goal is to have a *delighted customer* by providing all the expected results to an acceptable quality and standard. Fall short on the quality, budget, scope, delivery or performance standards expected and you will only create a complaining customer. This is potentially a lost customer in the future, which is bad news for the organization and your track record! A disgruntled customer is not too easy to convince that they should accept a cost over-run.

Customers also expect you and your project team to serve them with professional competence. You must ensure the right people with experience and appropriate skills are assigned to the project work, behave in a cooperative and friendly manner and demonstrate a real concern to meet the customer's expectations.

Always take your customer seriously – your project may be labelled as a failure if the deliverables are never utilized, under-utilized or even completely misutilized by the customer.

IDENTIFYING THE PROJECT CONSTRAINTS

In today's business environment it is rare for you to have unlimited resources, funding and time to complete the work. The project may yield significantly reduced benefits if you provide the results at a time when the requirements or the market needs have changed dramatically. If the outcome of your project is a new business service to others, the marketing people will have derived a business case with forecasts of potential market development. This case will have also identified some critical dates for effective implementation to realize the business potential. The PST will inevitably ask many questions about the potential and key dates to realize the business benefits. If customers are also involved they may have already created expectations that will benefit their business.

DEFINITION

A constraint is a limiting condition, circumstance or event, setting boundaries for the project process and expected outcomes.

Identifying the project constraints is critical at this stage of the decision process. Failure to identify or ignore an important constraint can have seriously damaging consequences.

Business and market needs are continually changing. Even with an internal project, late completion may lead others to conclude the whole effort was a waste of time, because of new requirements. Project 'drift' sets in and you face what seems like a never-ending project, trapped into acquiring a legacy of the 'project manager with the endless project'.

Constraints usually fall into categories:

- Financial – project cost, capital costs, materials, revenue and resource costs.

- Environmental – management conditions, working environment, processes.

- Time – time to deliver the results, the critical date when the results are needed.

- Quality – the scope, specifications and standards to be achieved.

Start to build a library of project and programme constraints you meet in your project work and use this as a checklist. Identifying constraints is a team activity and must include some of the key stakeholders. When you have compiled the constraint list, make a table as shown in Figure 4.4 and agree by consensus what the level of impact is likely to be based on present knowledge. Assign a high, medium or low impact to each constraint.

Record the name of the team member assigned responsibility for monitoring. The focus will be on high and medium impact constraints just like risks (see Chapter 7) but the impact may change so do not ignore the low impact constraints. A common problem is to identify assumptions as constraints, so it is important to define the constraint carefully. For example, at this early stage of a project to be given a budget is always an assumption. Without any planning the costs and budget cannot be derived.

KEY FACT

Constraints are roadblocks to achieving success so focus on developing mitigation workaround strategies for all major constraints.

Another feature of many constraints is their point(s) of impact in the project schedule. Some constraints may only really impact the work at specific stages and each potential point of impact must be determined and recorded in the schedule documentation. It is important that the team member with monitoring responsibility for each constraint reviews the plan before it is approved by the PST and identifies the most likely points of impact. Then the team

CONSTRAINT NAME	IMPACT			MONITORING RESPONSIBLITY
	HIGH	MEDIUM	LOW	
FINANCIAL CONSTRAINTS				
Project cost must not exceed a given figure				
Project capital budget is restricted to a given figure				
Key team members available on part-time basis only				
Some team members will not have relevant technical experience				
The customer has limited staff with relevant experience to support project team				
Budget for co-locating project team members is limited				
The approved supplier list for key materials is restricted				
ENVIRONMENTAL CONSTRAINTS				
Some or all senior management have limited experience and/or knowledge of project management processes				
Senior management are not in agreement to initiate the project				
An overtime ban is in effect and will restrict team to normal working hours				
TIME CONSTRAINTS				
Phase completion dates have been fixed by Marketing Department				
Handover to Sales Department has been fixed before plan development				
Key customers have been promised availability before plan approval				
QUALITY CONSTRAINTS				
Scope creep is inevitable because of project unknowns				
Customer quality standards are not acceptable				
Customer will revise specifications as project proceeds				

Figure 4.4 Constraint management table

can identify what workaround(s) if any can be derived and inserted in the plan.

You need to explore each with your key stakeholders to gather the information you need to guarantee success. You will find that the customer will often be unable to answer your questions, arguing that it is part of the project work for you to uncover the answers.

 KEY FACT

It is essential to review constraints at least at each phase gate. As climate conditions change new constraints can appear and old ones can change in impact.

For a further discussion on constraints and risks, refer to Chapter 7.

ASSUMPTIONS

An assumption is an educated 'guess' based on information that is presumed to be true in the absence of any certainty. Being given a budget creates a belief there are adequate funds to complete the project on time. This assumption is not based on any plan or demonstrated budget estimate – it is clearly a 'back of the envelope calculation'. However if you need to modify the scope and adapt the schedule to meet the specified budget, this now becomes a serious constraint.

Assumptions are potential sources of future roadblocks, so ensure that you do record them now and in the future as more get made.

At some point in your project you must validate every assumption or they will become issues to be resolved. The assumptions have no value later as excuses for failing to do something because either you or someone else forgot that it had been assumed and it was never recorded. Assumptions should be evaluated from a long-term perspective by asking two questions for each assumption:

- 'How confident are we that this assumption will be proven correct?'
- 'If proven correct what will be the likely consequences for the project?'

By answering these questions you can assess the impact on the project, from serious (real threat to timely, successful completion) to minor (insignificant impact). Based on the confidence level and impact you can decide what action to take now or review at a later date. High confidence that an assumption is true suggests no further analysis is needed; low confidence and high impact does need further analysis and such assumptions are very likely to become a risk.

It is important that the PST is given a summary of the analysis and what assumptions have been made to help it with decision processing. It is easy in a climate that encourages you to get going with the project to ignore assumptions and just take the view: 'We'll deal with that later'.

KEY FACT

Assumptions that are ignored inevitably become Issues that must be resolved to avoid impacting project progress.

REVIEW AND CONTROL

The constraints and assumptions identified in the early stages of a project are never static. As the work of the project proceeds assumptions will be proven true or untrue and constraints may change quite dramatically. Just as these features of the project are similar to risks you must be prepared to react promptly with mitigation plans, contingencies, workarounds or revisions to plans, schedules and even possibly the project scope. Recording constraints and assumptions is not enough; they must be tracked and monitored throughout the whole project life cycle with careful monitoring of the impact points in the plan and when appropriate action plans derived. This is an essential ingredient of the control process (see Chapter 9).

Once the project is complete you will be required to conduct a post-project evaluation. This includes a review of the risks and issues and their management during the project. At the same time ensure you evaluate the assumptions and constraints in the same manner and review how these were managed. Evaluate the actions taken to identify, analyse, incorporate, monitor and control considering the accuracy, effectiveness and timing. The data from such evaluation and review will improve project management in your organization and contribute to a successful outcome.

THE KICK-OFF MEETING

Hold a kick-off meeting. This meeting is the first time you collect together the team with other key people who have an interest in the project. It is an opportunity for you to demonstrate your ability to lead the project team. Good preparation is important to achieve the meeting purpose. Avoid diving into too much detail at this stage – that will come later. Focusing on one area in detail will divert the meeting and not fulfil the meeting purpose.

The project sponsor should chair and open the meeting to explain the strategic context of the proposed project. Explain why the project is important now and how it is ranked in contrast to other active projects. Your purpose is to gain as much information as possible at this stage by asking questions.

Issue an agenda to give attendees time to prepare. Keep the attendee list down to a minimum where possible.

Some typical questions to ask at the kick-off meeting include:

BACKGROUND

- Why is the project necessary?
- What is the overall problem or opportunity being addressed?
- Has the current situation been explored and understood?
- Has a statement of requirements been derived from the needs list?
- Is this an old problem?
- How long has it existed?
- Who wants to change things?
- Have previous attempts (projects) been made to address this problem?
- What information exists about past attempts to fix things?
- What assumptions have been made?

CONTEXT

- Is the project in line with current organizational strategy?
- Will the project form part of a chain of linked projects or a programme?
- What is the timescale of the project?
- Is there a business critical date to get the results?
- Will the results be of value to another customer or part of the organization?

APPROACH

- Have all the needs been identified and analysed?
- Has a statement of requirements been agreed?
- Are there predetermined solutions?
- What are these solutions?
- Is there a best option and a least worst option?
- Is there enough time to explore more than one option?
- Are there known checkpoints for project review other than the phase gates?
- What specialized skills are expected to be required for the project work?

OBJECTIVES

- Are the project primary deliverables known?
- What does the customer need, want and wish to get from the project?
- Can these deliverables be clearly defined and specified?
- Does the end user agree with these deliverables?
- What does the end user need, want and wish to get from the project?
- What are the perceived project benefits?
- Have these benefits been quantified?
- Has a project budget been fixed?
- Is capital investment necessary?
- Has a capital expenditure request been initiated?

- Is time used for project work to be measured and costed?
- How were the costs derived?
- Has a cost–benefit analysis been carried out?
- Has a financial appraisal been carried out to establish payback?

CONSTRAINTS

- Have the project constraints been identified and analyzed?
- Is there a time constraint for all or part of the deliverables list?
- Are there any financial constraints, for example manufacture cost, project cost?
- Is there a financial payback constraint?
- Are there any known technical constraints, for example, new or untried technology?
- Are there known resource constraints?
- Is the project team to be located together on one site?
- Is part of the work to be carried out at another site?
- Is part of the work to be carried out by sub-contractors or suppliers?
- Is there a preferred list of approved sub-contractors and suppliers?
- What existing specifications and standards are to be applied to the project?
- Are there any legal constraints that might affect the project work?
- Are there any security implications?
- Are there any operational constraints, for example access to production areas/test equipment, etc?
- Are there any Health and Safety constraints?

The data collected from these and other questions you can add will help you prepare a comprehensive business case. Your objective is to create a document that demonstrates:

- a clear understanding of the customer needs;
- what you can achieve to satisfy those needs;
- an assessment of the potential risks;
- what benefits the project could provide the organization;
- an indication of the timescales involved;
- an assessment of the costs and return on investment involved.

The business case is not a one-off exercise as you will be required to review, validate and update, if appropriate, the contents at each phase gate until the project is complete.

RECORDING ESSENTIAL INFORMATION

You are not alone – no one likes having to record information in a regular and organized manner. Project work produces a large amount of data and it is important that you record essential material. One of the greatest timewasters in project work is repeating the recording of information in different formats and the problems created in its interpretation later. If your organization is regularly carrying out projects then it is valid to establish a Project Data Repository (PDR) for all project documentation. This will ensure that even when paper copies of documents are in circulation, there is always a copy of the latest version in the PDR. The principal inputs to the PDR are shown in Figure 4.5.

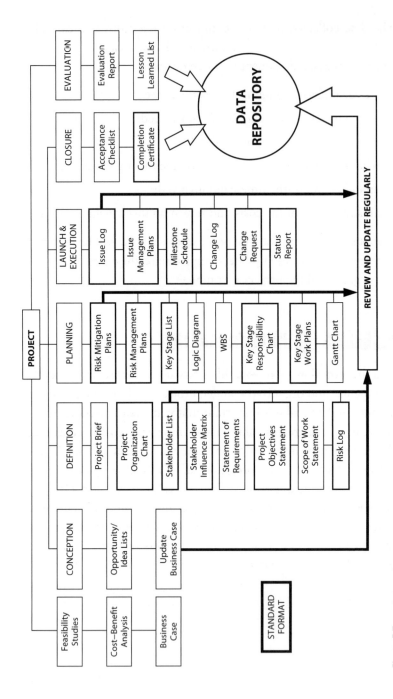

Figure 4.5 Project data repository inputs

For this process to be successful many of the regularly used documents for project work should be designed as standard formats with strict version control on each issue. This approach has two key benefits:

- Each format contains the essential information required for project control.
- Each format has an owner who is responsible for document version control.

Examples of some of these standard formats are given in the subsequent chapters. Other documents produced during the project such as the Business Case or Scope of Work Statement is unique to each project but they can still be produced using a standardized template. The principal documents employed are shown in Figure 4.6.

Every document or standard format produced throughout the project process must have an owner who is responsible for:

- ensuring each format is completed with accuracy and due diligence;
- ensuring the new issue of a document or format is signed off appropriately for issue;
- maintaining and controlling the distribution list;
- issuing the document and controlling issue numbers;
- maintaining strict version control recording all changes made.

As the project manager you are responsible for all project documentation, but in practice you cannot complete, issue and control all the paper so assign some of this responsibility to team members. Draw up a documentation table as shown in Figure 4.5 that shows ownership, version control and issue distribution lists. As project manager you own this document and must update it and reissue regularly throughout the project as each document is issued for the first time. Risk Mitigation Plans forms and Issue Management Plans forms are included for completeness and ownership for

PROJECT DOCUMENT PLAN					Issue No: 1	Date:	
TITLE:							
SPONSOR:		PROJECT MANAGER:			CUSTOMER:		
DOC. No.	DOCUMENT		VERSION No.	ISSUE No.	DISTRIBUTION (Enter initials)		OWNER
01	Feasibility Study						
02	Cost–Benefit Analysis						
03	Business Case						
04	Project Brief						
05	Project Organization Chart						
06	Stakeholder List						
07	Stakeholder Influence Matrix						
08	Statement of Requirements						
09	Project Objectives Statement						
10	Scope of Work Statement						
11	Risk Log						
12	Risk Mitigation Plan(s)						
13	Risk Management Plan(s)						
14	Key Stage List						
15	Key Stage Responsibility Chart						
16	Key Stage Work Plans						
17	Gantt Chart						
18	Issue Log						
19	Issue Management Plan(s)						
20	Milestone Schedule						
21	Change Log						
22	Change Request						
23	Status Report						
24	Acceptance Checklist						
25	Completion Certificate						
APPROVALS:		DATE	PREPARED BY:			DATE:	
SPONSOR							
PROJECT MANAGER							

Figure 4.6 Example project document table

version control, but the formats are issued by the risk and issue owners, respectively. It is valid to issue the Project Document Table to all team members and key stakeholders at the kick-off meeting when you should stress that you consider only these documents as the official project documentation that will be registered in the PDR as they are issued. Stress that no other documents are to be put into circulation unless they have been approved and added to the Project Document Table. It is a valid to give one of your team responsibility for configuration management to ensure there is always good version control of all documents in current use.

SUMMARY

Ensure you understand:

- The steps involved in effective project selection
- The initial approval steps to the start of project definition
- The importance of building a strong working relationship with your customer
- How to identify constraints and assumptions with your team
- The essential need to:
  - Hold a kick-off meeting
  - Establish a project data repository where all the team uses standard data recording formats and procedures.

5

THE DEFINITION PHASE

THE PROJECT BRIEF AND SPECIFICATION

Now that the PST has given approval to pass through Phase gate 1 you can start work on the project definition.

The data you collect from the kick-off meeting should enable you to draw up a preliminary statement of the project objectives and the associated specifications. This step is often the most difficult because you must now formulate in realistic terms just what the project is about and what it has to achieve. This is the foundation of project definition.

The *project brief* is a document that summarizes all the relevant facts about the project and is, therefore, a source of definitive information. The contents include:

- the project origins – a need or opportunity statement;
- the project rationale – why is it necessary now?

- the benefits of the project – to the customer and your organization;
- the project budget if known at this stage;
- the current timescale and expected deadlines – subject always to detailed planning later.

This document is ideally just one piece of paper, but for larger projects it often takes the form of a report with many different sections. The former is best as it forces you and the team to focus on real facts and not hopes or wishes. Unfortunately during the start-up of most projects there is too much expression of hopes and the 'wish list'. You have to resolve this conflict to sort out what you can achieve in practice with current technology, experience and knowledge that is compatible with the statement of requirements.

The project specification is a term applied to many different types of documents and can include almost anything. Here the term specification describes any document that is an obligatory statement of processes, procedures and standards that apply to the project. It is a statement of policy for the project.

KEY FACT

The Project Brief is an executive summary of your project which with the business case creates a project charter.

DEFINING THE PROJECT

You may ask at this point, 'What is the difference between start-up and definition?' The first is a data gathering activity. Definition is the process of turning the data into something that is no longer just a wish or a hope. Failure to give adequate time to this activity and derive all the relevant data for this foundation will lead to a poorly defined project with a considerably reduced chance of achieving a successful outcome.

WHAT IS NECESSARY TO DEFINE A PROJECT?

This definition phase is where many projects go wrong – often because there is no clear definition or it has remained confused with so many different stakeholder inputs. Remember successful definition must involve all the team at every step, to build their acceptance and commitment to the work of the project.

EXERCISE

Having conducted a kick-off meeting what do you need to write down now to define your project? List what you consider is essential information:

_____

_____

_____

_____

_____

_____

_____

Everyone has their own ideas about what constitutes a definition but your purpose here is to ensure that everyone understands:

- what you intend to provide from the project;
- what you do not intend to provide;
- when the outcomes are to be provided;
- what constraints you have identified;
- what risks are involved.

Is this what you have written down? Your objective now is to:

- use the data gathered about customer needs and expectations;
- turn these needs into requirements – what you believe satisfies the needs;
- derive a project definition to specify these requirements;
- ask your customer to approve this definition.

KEY FACT

The project definition must be agreed, approved and 'signed off' by the Customer and Sponsor before any time is spent on planning.

Before you call the team together to define the project open the business-case document and review the initial data recorded. Some details may now have changed and you will need to draw any variances to the attention of the PST when you have completed the definition. The definition process is given in Figure 5.1.

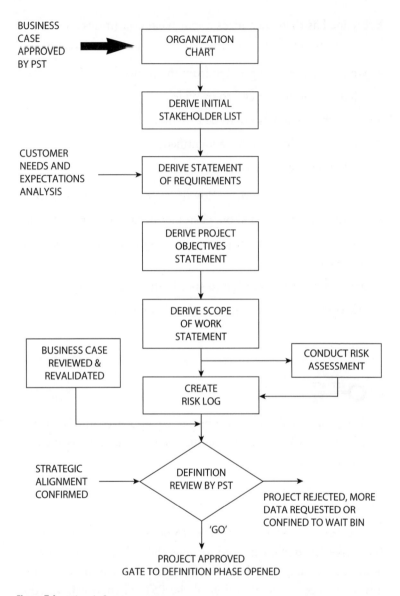

Figure 5.1 The definition process

A PROJECT ORGANIZATION CHART

Draw up a list to show who is involved in the project, recording:

- name and job title/position;
- location;
- contact telephone/fax number and e-mail address;
- date assigned to the project;
- name of their line manager and contact data;
- distribution list.

Date the document and issue to everyone who needs to know – this is an essential communication document for resource planning. It ensures there is clarity about who is committed to the project. Ensure the line managers of everyone in the team receive this information – they are stakeholders and need to confirm their commitment by agreeing to these new assignments.

A STAKEHOLDER LIST

Identify all those with an interest in the project – the stakeholders. The identification and management of stakeholders is a key activity for your success. It is suggested you read though Chapter 6 now before proceeding any further with definition. Create a stakeholder list, recording:

- name of stakeholder and job title/position;
- location and contact data (telephone/fax/e-mail);
- whether internal/external to your organization;
- ranking of importance to the project (high, medium, low);
- current degree of support for the project (positive, negative?).

Date this document because it is subject to change as you review the list at regular intervals. Ensure the list is distributed to all stakeholders. An example format for a single page organization chart and stakeholder list is shown in Figure 5.2.

It is important that all single format data recording formats carry similar project data in the upper and lower sections.

PROJECT ORGANIZATION CHART				Issue No: 1	Date:	
TITLE:						
SPONSOR:		PROJECT MANAGER:			CUSTOMER:	
NAME MANAGER	PROJECT ROLE	DEPARTMENT	ASSIGNED	TEL No.		LINE
APPROVALS:		DATE	PREPARED BY:		DATE:	
SPONSOR			DISTRIBUTION:			
PROJECT MANAGER						

PROJECT STAKEHOLDER LIST				Issue No: 1	Date:			
TITLE:								
SPONSOR:	PROJECT MANAGER:				CUSTOMER:			
STAKEHOLDER NAME		TEL. No.	INT	EXT	HIGH	MEDIUM	LOW	(+)	(−)
APPROVALS:		DATE						
SPONSOR			DISTRIBUTION:					
PROJECT MANAGER								

Figure 5.2 Example project organization chart and stakeholder list

A STATEMENT OF REQUIREMENTS

From the needs and expectations derived from your discussions with the stakeholders derive the data for this document. This must involve all the team to decide just what can be provided to satisfy the needs and may take several meetings. The document should record:

- needs and expectations identified and to whom attributed;
- how these needs can be met in practice;
- which needs cannot be satisfied yet and why;
- what assumptions have been made at this stage;
- what the project is about and what is not included.

The statement must always be qualified as being based on available information at the date of preparation as new data may become available later.

A PROJECT OBJECTIVES STATEMENT

The information recorded here must be derived working with your customer recording:

- the overall project objective – in 25–30 words;
- the primary deliverables of the project with expected delivery dates;
- the primary benefits to be gained – quantified financially in the business case;
- the anticipated cost of the project;
- what skills are required – particularly those not currently available;
- any identified interfaces with other active projects.

Ensure all deliverables and benefits satisfy the SMART test:

SPECIFIC – clearly defined with completion criteria;

MEASURABLE – understood metrics are available to identify delivery;

ACHIEVABLE – within the current environment and skills available;

REALISTIC – not trying to get the impossible with many unknowns;

TIMEBOUND – is limited by a delivery date based on real need.

The project objectives statement is the foundation of your project, listing out the key deliverables and benefits to be achieved and their expected delivery dates. The document can also include an overall objectives statement as a summary along with proposed and required completion dates – remember the project has not been fully approved or planned so dates are forecasts only at this stage. Figure 5.3 shows an example of a typical project objectives statement.

The document must be approved by the PST and signed off by the project sponsor and any subsequent revisions must be signed off by the project sponsor.

It is also valid to identify any important aspects of your proposed strategy for the project, eg:

- examining several options;
- using sub-contractors for part of the work (where skills are missing);
- using consultants for support and advice;
- re-using known methods, processes or technology.

This data can be included if required although it is common for it to be included in the scope of work statement.

PROJECT OBJECTIVES STATEMENT		Issue No: 1		Date:	

TITLE:		PROJECT NUMBER:			
SPONSOR:	PROJECT MANAGER:		CUSTOMER:		

NAME	PROJECT ROLE	DEPARTMENT	TEL. No.	LINE MANAGER

PROPOSED START DATE: REQUIRED COMPLETION DATE:

OVERALL OBJECTIVE STATEMENT:

DELIVERABLES	EXPECTED DATE

BENEFITS	EXPECTED DATE

RESOURCE SKILLS REQUIRED:	RELATED TO OTHER PROJECT/PROGRAMME? ◯ Y ◯ N REFERENCE NUMBER:

FORECAST COST: RISK LOG ATTCHED: ◯ Y ◯ N

APPROVALS:	DATE	PREPARED BY:	DATE:		
SPONSOR		DISTRIBUTION:			
PROJECT MANAGER					

Figure 5.3 Example content of the project objectives statement

A SCOPE OF WORK STATEMENT

DEFINITION

The Scope of Work statement is a narrative description of the project objectives in more detail with expanded information about each expected deliverable and their associated benefits.

The document must also clearly identify the boundary limits of the project, stating unequivocally what is not going to be done as part of the project.

This is a convenient place to record other useful data and cross-references to past reports and relevant projects. The document also includes:

- the project boundary limits identified – what you are not going to do;
- the standards and specifications that are applicable;
- internal product specifications;
- external product specifications;
- mandatory standards imposed by legislation;
- process specifications;
- customer specifications;
- standard operating procedures;
- purchasing procedures;
- quality standards;
- testing specifications and procedures;

- sub-contract terms and conditions imposed on third parties;
- any exceptions to these standards;
- where the standards and specifications are kept for reference;
- how success is to be measured;
- constraints identified and possible workarounds.
- assumptions made to date in the project.

The scope of work statement is a useful place to locate any other relevant information that supports and clarifies your definition. It is valid to include references to other documents that may have been prepared earlier on the project, for example:

- cost–benefit analysis;
- feasibility report(s);
- business case;
- reports from independent consultants.

RISK ASSESSMENT

There are risks to all projects and *risk management* is a method of managing a project that focuses on identifying and controlling the areas or events that have the potential of creating and causing unwanted change leading to unwanted results. Risk management must not be considered as a separate function that you 'do' at the start-up and then leave the results in a drawer; it is an integral part of project methodology. Because of the complexity of risks it is impossible to derive a universal process for managing all risks in a project. But we can achieve a high level of control and successful management of risks with some simple and well tested techniques that can be used in most situations to help you achieve project success. What is a risk?

A risk assessment at this stage of a project may kill the project – through identifying such a high level of risk compared to other potential projects that it is not good business sense to continue. Three fundamental categories of risks are always present:

- *business risks* – the viability and context of the project;
- *project risks* – associated with the technical aspects of the work to achieve the required outcomes;
- *process risks* – associated with the project process, procedures, tools and techniques employed to control the project.

As project manager, it is your obligation, working with your team, to:

- identify and evaluate potential risks;
- obtain agreement to action plans to contain the risks;
- take the actions and monitor the results;
- promptly resolve any issues arising from risks that happen.

KEY FACT

All projects inherently contain risk by default. Your success is dependent on how well you manage the risks throughout the project.

KEEP YOUR HEAD – DON'T GO WILD!

Project managers often complain that risk management is negative and an infinite process – you do not have to try too hard to come up with an enormous list of potential risks. There is no real value in listing risks you know just cannot be controlled by you or your team. Do not list 'acts of God' such as war, flood, earthquakes etc. Similarly many perceived risks in the economy and marketplace will have an eventual consequence for you but you cannot control these directly. Risk identification is highly dependent on individual perception and clearly some measure of judgement must be exercised when listing such risks to focus on those that may have a rapid and direct impact on your project. Then you can decide any mitigation action you could recommend if they seem likely to occur.

Chapter 6 is devoted to the process involved in management of risks.

WHEN IS IT NECESSARY?

Risk management is a *continuous process* throughout the life cycle of the project and you must keep all the team focused on the risks:

- start now at the definition phase;
- it is essential to establishing the definition;
- compile a complete list as a project risk log.

An example project risk log is shown in Figure 5.4. At this stage you only list the risks identified and assign ownership for each risk to one of your team members. This ensures every potential risk is monitored for impact and likelihood of actually affecting the project progress. Later you will carry out a rigorous review of each risk to analyze the impact on the project. This is discussed in detail in Chapter 7.

PROJECT RISK LOG

| | | | | | Page | of | | Issue No: 1 | | Date: |

TITLE:

PROJECT NUMBER:

SPONSOR: **PROJECT MANAGER:**

PLANNED START DATE:

PLANNED COMPLETION DATE:

RISK DATA

No;	CATEGORY U/H/M/L	TITLE	DATE RAISED	ACTIVITY ID	COST 000's	TYPE T/A/R	STATUS A/C/T/S	SCORE P	I	S	RMP Y/N	RMF Y/N	OWNER

APPROVALS:	DATE:	PREPARED BY:	DATE:
SPONSOR		DISTRIBUTION:	
PROJECT MANAGER			

NOTES: 1. RISK CATEGORY – U: unacceptable. H: high. M: medium. L: low   3. RISK STATUS – A: active. C: completed. T: cancelled. S: suspended
2. RISK TYPE – T: transfer. A: avoidance. R: residual   4. RISK SCORE – P: PROBABILITY. I : IMPACT. S: RISK SCORE

Figure 5.4 Example project risk log

The *project risk log* will need to be reviewed at regular intervals, normally monthly at project progress meetings. This review process focuses on:

- any change in the potential impact or probability of identified risks;
- any risks changed from previously lower ranking, which are then subjected to closer examination;
- deriving contingency plans for either avoidance and/or damage limitation;
- adding any new risks identified to the list and assessing these for impact and probability.

A risk entered on the list is never removed, even if the time zone when it could occur has passed. Your list of risks is a source of valuable learning data for future projects and is a useful data source for deriving checklists.

GETTING YOUR PROJECT DEFINITION APPROVED

Start by checking you have done everything you can at this stage to clearly define the project by ensuring you have answers to the questions in the check list.

CHECKLIST NO 5 – DEVELOPING THE DEFINITION

- Is the project organization clearly established?
- Is the customer identified?
- Are roles and responsibilities at all levels understood and accepted?
- Are project accountability and authority statements issued?

- Is the corporate and strategic context and priority of the project understood?

- Has a Project Organization Chart been prepared and issued?

- Has a Statement of Requirements been derived?

- Has the Project Stakeholder List been prepared and issued?

- Have stakeholder management responsibilities been assigned in the team?

- Has a project need/purpose/opportunity statement been agreed?

- Has all the relevant background information been collected?

- Is there an agreed overall Project Objective Statement?

- Is there a Business Critical date for the completion of the project?

- Are the project deliverables clearly identified?

- Have the project benefits been established?

- Have the project approach and strategy been agreed?

- Is the project related to other projects?

- Have the project risks been identified and quantified so far?

- Has a Project Risk Log been prepared?

- Have the identified risks been assigned owners?

- Has a Scope of Work Statement been prepared?

- Have the project constraints been identified and analysed?

- Have all assumptions made so far been documented clearly?

- Are existing communication procedures acceptable for the project?

- Has the alignment with current strategy been confirmed?

- Has the business case been reviewed and updated where necessary?

- Has a Project Brief been prepared ready for approval?

- Has the date for presentation to the PST been agreed?

Now you can seek approval of your sponsor and customer. If possible use the opportunity to hold a team and stakeholder meeting for this definition review. Hold a team and stakeholder meeting to review and agree the project definition. The sponsor will present the outcome to the PST for them to approve the definition and open the entry gate to the planning phase. This approval opens the way for planning effort to proceed.

SUMMARY

To effectively define your project:

- Establish and record the project organization
- Identify and record the stakeholder list
- Derive a statement of requirements and an objectives statement
- Draw up a scope of work statement
- Conduct a risk assessment
- Record the risks identified

Then seek customer and sponsor approval of your project definition.

MANAGING THE STAKEHOLDERS

WHAT IS A STAKEHOLDER?

In Chapter 2 we identified the stakeholder as anyone who can find reason to have an interest, however direct or indirect, in your project. These individuals who may act independently or represent groups consider they have a right to influence your project in some way. Ignore them at your peril.

EXERCISE

Think about your last project and list all the people other than the project team who exerted some influence on the project objectives, work content or progress at some time during the project.

How many have you identified in just a few minutes? Now you can see that there could be many of these influencers working in the project environment. Although you may not readily accept the fact, you cannot avoid them and they will always exist.

KEY FACT

Success is directly related to the effective management of the project stakeholders as part of the project process.

At the end of the project who really decides whether it has been successful? Yes, it's the key stakeholders:

- your customer;
- your sponsor;
- the customer's user group;
- the Finance department.

They will soon let you know if they consider the project met their expectations or conversely if you have failed. As they are frequently an ignored group, that justifies us devoting this chapter to stakeholder management as a key step to good practice on the success ladder.

The importance of the stakeholders

It is essential to identify all the stakeholders as early as possible in the project life. Failure to engage them may be fatal. Never underestimate the ability of any stakeholder to ruin your plans through use of their power and influence.

All the stakeholders have an open and a closed or hidden agenda about what they expect from your project. You need to expose these expectations before you finalize the definition of the project and agree the scope. This is not easy when there is a political dimension affecting their needs and expectations – one need could be to hinder or stop the project if it impacts on their sphere of influence! The relative importance of each changes with time and the progress of the project, and they may change their support to outright hindrance at any time if it benefits them as individuals.

IDENTIFYING STAKEHOLDERS

Identifying stakeholders is not just part of the project start-up. As many appear later, you must review the list at regular intervals. The relative importance of each changes with time and through the stages of the project. It is a serious risk to fail to cooperate with or recognize a stakeholder. Set the ground rules at the outset – poor stakeholder control will lead to chaos and demotivation of your team!

The stakeholders are inside and outside your organization. It is a good idea to ask your sponsor and customer to get involved in the activity of stakeholder identification since some stakeholders impact both.

List out all the functions that are expected to have an influence or interest in your project and then identify the individual (particularly the resource managers) in each function with whom you need to have a conversation about their specific interest. Stakeholders could come from any of the following:

- Finance department;
- Sales and Marketing department;
- Development department;
- Strategic Planning department;
- Production department;
- consultants;
- contractors;
- suppliers;
- supply chain third parties; other divisions or sites;
- statutory bodies;
- government agencies;
- the public.

With the team start by thinking about the people:

- whom you need to take with you through the project;
- who will be affected in some way by the project at any stage;
- who will be quietly watching what you are doing in the project.

Then ask:

1 Who are the primary customer, secondary customer and sponsor?

2 Who decided that this programme/project should proceed?

3 Which organizations, divisions, functions have an interest?

4 Which sites will be involved?

5 Who on each site is likely to be a key stakeholder?

6 Is any other organization likely to be involved?

7 Who external has an interest?

8 Who is likely to directly influence the work of this programme/project?

9 Who is likely to indirectly influence the work of this programme/project?

10 Who is likely to be directly affected by the work and/or outcomes of this programme/project?

11 Who is likely to be indirectly affected by the work and or outcomes of this programme/project?

12 Who are likely to be observers who could choose to influence this programme/project?

On the first pass put everyone you think of on your list. You can clean up the list later to focus on those who will have the most impact. It is not uncommon for a project to be initiated in an organization without any internal communication occurring. Ensure you agree with your sponsor what communication needs to occur to let others know you have started a new project and what it is intended to achieve.

THE TWO MOST IMPORTANT STAKEHOLDERS

The project sponsor

This is normally the person who gave you responsibility for the project. In Chapter 1 we defined this person as having account-ability for the project on behalf of the organization. This is not just a nominal role because the individual happens to be a senior manager. Many projects run into difficulties because the sponsor does not fulfil the obligations of the role.

A key success factor is the continued engagement of the project Sponsor, the individual who has the authority to make decisions about resources – the money and people you need to get the job done.

The sponsor cannot be effective if the individual has no authority in the organization. Most organizations today still maintain a reluctance to give their project managers enough authority to get the job done.

The sponsor is accountable for the project and therefore is the appointed guardian of the project on behalf of the organization. You should demand delegation of the authority you need to get the day-to-day work of the project done on time.

An effective sponsor can also provide you with a significant amount of support through:

- responding rapidly to issues requiring senior management decisions;
- sustaining the agreed priority of the project in the organization;
- sustaining the project direction to avoid subtle enhancements of scope – scope 'creep';
- ensuring the project stays focused on the organization's strategic needs;
- building a working relationship with the customer;
- influencing the peer group to provide cross-organization resources and services on time for the project;
- demonstrating concern for success by visible leadership;
- influencing other stakeholders in the approval and sign-off of the phases of the project.

These are the essential responsibilities of the sponsor's role in project work. You need to start out with the intention of building a good working relationship with your sponsor to benefit from this support. Agree that you will meet face to face regularly – preferably once a week, if only for 20 minutes.

THE CUSTOMER

Clearly identify who really is your customer and who is your main contact since you must start to build a working relationship with this individual. Many projects have multiple customers, outside or even inside the organization. Customers have personal perceptions of what they want from your project and if there is a wide variance in these perceptions hostility and conflict may be generated. You need to use all your skills of diplomacy to influence such a group and identify the needs and expectations of each customer.

Ask the key questions:

Who is your primary customer?

If you have more than one, who are they?

Who are the main contacts for each customer?

Add contact details for each customer contact – e-mail, telephone number.

Add these stakeholders to a standardized listing of all stakeholders.

If you have multiple customers get them to agree that one of the group takes the role of customer representative. The customer representative is the key individual who has the necessary authority to take decisions affecting the project. Preferably this should not be a committee.

STAKEHOLDER INFLUENCE

As you start to build the stakeholder list for both the customer organization and your organization, consider:

- Who wants you to succeed?
- Who might want you to fail?
- Who will visibly support the project?
- Who will visibly hinder or oppose your project?
- Who will invisibly support the project?
- Who will invisibly hinder or oppose the project?
- Who will benefit from the project?
- Who will lose something because of the project?
- Whose success is impacted by the project?
- Whose success is enhanced by the project?

Depending on the type of project it may be valid to ask:

- Whom can I ignore as the project progresses?
- Whom can I not ignore as the project progresses?

Covert criticism or interference can quickly demotivate the team, destroy team spirit and promote conflict. Poor stakeholder control can lead to chaos, confusion and frustration in your team through this perceived interference. Now you have a more comprehensive listing you can ask:

- What needs to be known about each stakeholder?
- Where and how can this information be gathered?
- What do we do with the data we collect?

GATHERING INFORMATION ABOUT STAKEHOLDERS

You will probably now have more stakeholders on your list than you ever thought possible. If you give them all equal time you will never get the project done so carefully examine the list and with your team agree:

- which stakeholders are critical to project success – key stakeholders;
- which stakeholders are best kept at a distance from the project;
- which stakeholders you are unable to influence at all.

Focus on the first category as a priority and start with the questions in Checklist 6.

CHECKLIST NO 6 – STAKEHOLDER INFORMATION

- What exactly is their interest?
- Why are they interested?
- What are they expecting to gain?
- What do they need?
- How will the project affect them?
- Can they contribute experience, knowledge or specific skills?
- What are their strengths and weaknesses?
- Are there likely to be hidden agendas and if so, what are they?
- What organizational authority does the stakeholder have?
- Do they have any legal rights?
- Are they openly in favour of the project?
- Will the project interfere with their operations?
- What might they lose because of the project?

- How could they hinder the project?
- Any history from previous projects?

Add any additional questions you can that are relevant to your project.

Eliminate any potential stakeholders you now consider will have a low or insignificant influence. Some will want to be listed for political reasons only, so take care they do not pop up later! Prepare a standard format to record your stakeholder list with the essential data derived. Leave some space for adding more data later after further analysis.

Once you have derived a more comprehensive listing of stakeholders with supporting data you can build an *influence matrix*.

THE STAKEHOLDER INFLUENCE MATRIX

Take your stakeholder list and categorize each stakeholder as one of four types:

- *decision maker* – one who provides resources or resolves issues.
- *direct influencer* – one with a direct input to the project work or is impacted by the project activities.
- *indirect influencer* – one with little or no direct input but may be needed to agree some actions to ensure success.
- *observer* – one who is apparently not affected by the project but may choose to try to impact your activities.

The matrix is shown in Figure 6.1.

For each stakeholder decide if they are:

- needed to provide resources?
- directly affected by the work?
- indirectly affected by the work?

- unaffected but have the power to affect the work should they choose to do so?

Discuss and agree with your team which category is applicable to each stakeholder, then enter a tick in the relevant category column with a polarity sign:

- a '+' sign for a stakeholder you consider positive about the project;
- a '–' sign for a stakeholder you consider clearly negative about the project;
- an 'N' for a stakeholder you consider is neutral about the project;
- a '?' for a stakeholder about whom you need to gather more data before deciding their position.

Use the information you derive to decide what you must do next. Decide which stakeholders you need to meet to get the information you are lacking to confirm your conclusions about each. Then you must decide what actions are necessary to influence the neutral and negative stakeholders. Remember you have a team and assign each member of the team one or more stakeholders to meet and gather information. You cannot afford to ignore these people. Give them respect in their role and you will get some surprises as you gather information. Your initial conclusions may be quite wrong so be prepared to receive new and unexpected data.

When you have gathered all the information you think necessary you will have a better idea who are the most important stakeholders with whom to maintain close contact.

KEY FACT

The Stakeholder List and Stakeholder Influence Matrix are never static and both documents must be subject to regular review and updating.

STAKEHOLDER INFLUENCE MATRIX

Project No:

NAME	ROLE	MANAGER	DECISION MAKER	DIRECT INFLUENCER	INDIRECT INFLUENCER	OBSERVER	OWNER
G. Trainer	Customer		✔ +			D.R.T.	
D. Foster	Sponsor		✔ +			D.R.T	
S. Strong	Technical Director			✔ +			J.K.D.
W. Storm	Service Manager				✔ N		G.R.
C. Isles	Sales Manager					?	W.T.G.
F. Willett	Dev. Manager			✔ –			D.F.R.
H. Grant	Prod. Manager			✔ N			G.R.
K. Driver	Stock Manager			?			S.C.H.
J. Fox	Chief Buyer			?			S.C.H.

Figure 6.1 The stakeholder influence matrix

WHAT HAPPENS NEXT WITH STAKEHOLDERS?

The list of stakeholders frequently changes as the project proceeds so expect new stakeholders to appear at any time. The key to good stakeholder management is effective communication. Decide how you intend to communicate with all the stakeholders; ask:

- what you need to tell:
  - the key stakeholders;
  - other stakeholders;
- how you will communicate with them;
- the frequency of the communication;
- how you will gather feedback.

Then tell them how and when they will receive this information but be cautious not to overload them. Busy people will not read long reports and they need short, objective reports that are of interest to them individually.

The key stakeholders you have identified will be expected to contribute to the project by getting involved in the reviews you need to conduct with your sponsor at various stages of the project. It is often relevant to hold short weekly review meetings with this small key group rather than the monthly all-day marathon meeting with a large group.

The continued commitment of all stakeholders is important for your success, so ensure you inform them at an early stage of that expectation. Many of the stakeholders may not be familiar with this approach to sustained involvement throughout a project. This ensures you can observe any changes in polarity where a disaffected stakeholder that was positive has become negative towards the project. Explain why this is important and that it will not demand a significant amount of time. Making them feel important is more likely to help rather than hinder you because of their remoteness.

SUMMARY

Understand the importance of stakeholders to your success.
Spend time with your team to:

- Identify all the stakeholders particularly your customer(s).
- Ask questions about each stakeholder to identify their potential influence.
- Use influence data to draw up an influence chart.
- Assign ownership of each stakeholder to a team member.
- Ensure stakeholder owners understand their responsibility and what is expected of them.
- Decide your strategy for communication with stakeholders.

MANAGING THE RISKS

Risk is an inherent property of any change activity and particularly projects. Risk management is the process of managing the uncertainty that always exists in project work and shows you the way to minimize or even avoid the 'show-stoppers' that can cost huge sums to correct. Every process and procedure in project management is aimed at minimizing risk and raising the probability of success. The skill is to identify the areas of high risk in a specific project and apply appropriate levels of monitoring and control.

WHAT IS A RISK?

DEFINITION

A risk is any uncertain event that, if it occurs, could prevent the project realizing the expectations of the stakeholders as stated in the agreed business case of project definition.

Every risk always has a cause and, if it occurs, a positive or negative consequence. A risk that becomes a reality is treated as an issue.

Effective Risk Management demands a high level of commitment to the risk management procedures described here. Your success as the Project Manager depends on encouraging a strong team commitment to always demonstrate their awareness of potential risks and their consequences. Many risks are latent, hidden deep in the schedule and plans and have a habit of appearing without warning. You must look for them before they impact your efforts unexpectedly at a time when you do not need such intervention.

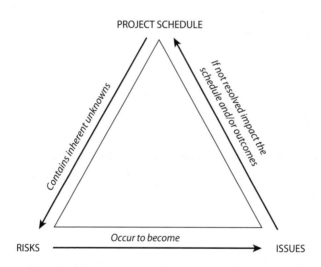

Figure 7.1 Impact of risk

WHY BOTHER?

Some consider risk management is a negative process, but consider the benefits:

- predicting the serious threats to your project before they happen;

- enabling mitigation actions to be implemented immediately;
- enabling contingency plans to be derived in advance;
- improved decision making in managing the project portfolio;
- providing valuable data for negotiating with suppliers and the marketplace;
- creating clear 'ownership' of the risks so they are carefully monitored;
- helping to create a 'no surprises' environment for the project;
- encouraging creativity and lateral thinking;
- encouraging decisive leadership rather than management of crisis.

Some will argue it is a costly activity – but never as costly as correcting the issues that occur later.

KEY FACT

Risk management is a vital and fundamental tool of project management that directly impacts your probability of success.

Application of a systematic process to risk management is not an option. Some small projects with unacceptably high levels of risk could easily impact other larger projects, so all projects should have a documented risk management activity.

As Figure 7.2 shows, increasing complexity and innovation with more cross-functional working increases the need for a structured approach to risk management.

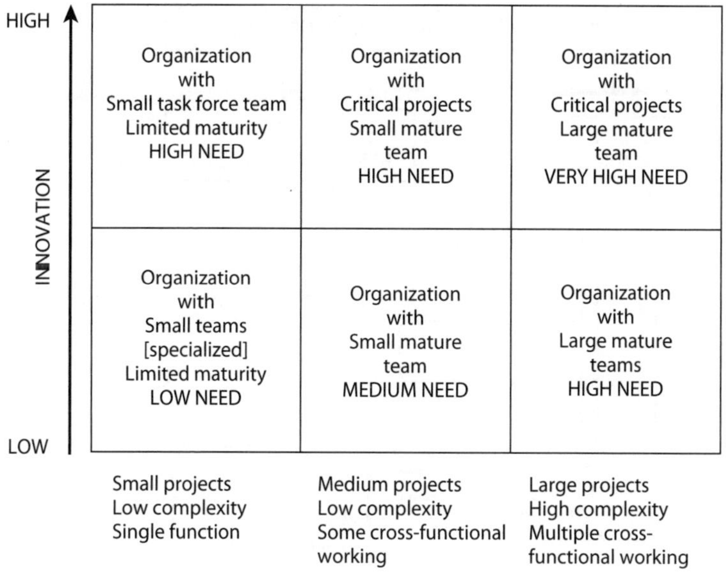
HIGH
LOW
INNOVATION
Organization with Small task force team Limited maturity HIGH NEED
Organization with Critical projects Small mature team HIGH NEED
Organization with Critical projects Large mature team VERY HIGH NEED
Organization with Small teams [specialized] Limited maturity LOW NEED
Organization with Small mature team MEDIUM NEED
Organization with Large mature teams HIGH NEED
Small projects Low complexity Single function
Medium projects Low complexity Some cross-functional working
Large projects High complexity Multiple cross-functional working

Figure 7.2 The need for risk management

THE RISK MANAGEMENT PROCESS

The process is shown in Figure 7.3. Your objective is to anticipate what could go wrong at any stage of the project and decide what can be done to avoid or correct the problem. Risk management is not a single-step process conducted only once. Unforeseen risks leading to unexpected issues demand prompt response so it is essentially a continuous process throughout the project until completion is recorded. All risks identified must be recorded on the Project Risk Log and never removed.

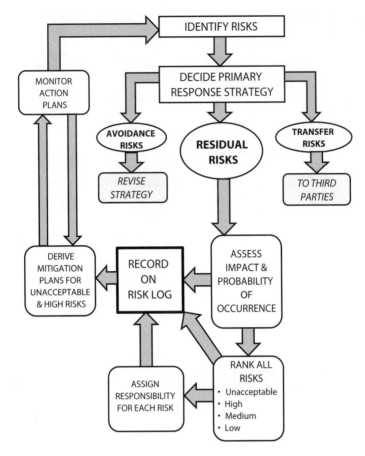

Figure 7.3 The risk management process

IDENTIFYING THE RISKS

Use a team brainstorming session to initially identify risks during the definition phase of the project. You are seeking an answer to the question: 'What could go wrong at any time during this project?' Engage your key stakeholders in the process. Involving the customer in the risk process has been shown to benefit everyone through agreeing the responsibilities for actions to avoid or mitigate a risk. You can also use checklists that have been developed from data generated from past projects. Never regard the checklist as complete or perfect (or just 'good enough') and additional questions are always necessary.

A TYPICAL STARTER CHECKLIST

CHECKLIST NO 7 – SOME QUESTIONS FOR RISK ASSESSMENT

If the answer is 'NO' then ask what needs to be done. Some questions apply to later stages of the project.

- Has the Project Sponsor clearly accepted the role? ☐
- Has the Project Manager's authority been established? ☐
- Is the core team appointed and released by their line manager? ☐
- Does the core team understand the Project purpose? ☐
- Have the project stakeholders been identified? ☐
- Have stakeholder management responsibilities been allocated? ☐
- Have the project objectives been established? ☐
- Have the project benefits been identified and quantified? ☐
- Are there clear deadlines and a project timescale? ☐
- Is there a known Business Critical Date for completion? ☐

- Is there a Scope of Work statement? ☐
- Are the project boundary limits clearly established? (What we are not going to do.) ☐
- Is there an impact if the project fails? ☐
- Are the right skills available in the team/organization? ☐
- Can the *Project Objectives Statement* be accurately derived? ☐
- Have all the project constraints been identified? ☐
- Are there identifiable consequences of late completion? ☐
- Has the *Project Definition* been approved? ☐
- Have all key stages been clearly identified? ☐
- Have key stage dependencies been established and agreed? ☐
- Are the key stage durations agreed and accepted? ☐
- Is the project schedule realistic and achievable? ☐
- Has a milestone schedule been established? ☐
- Have key stage responsibilities been allocated and accepted? ☐
- Are the resources realistically available? ☐
- Have workload priorities been clearly established? ☐
- Have line managers accepted and committed their staff involvement? ☐
- Have all resources required given commitment to their responsibilities? ☐
- Have project procedures been established and understood ☐

Review the initial list and remove duplicates, then ask what is impacted if the risk happens. Is it any of:

1 cost – the overall cost of the work;

2 schedule – the time the project will take;

3 scope – the project deliverables and quality of the work?

If there is no impact on these three elements then ask if it really is a risk in your project.

This is where you must use judgement to focus the risks to those you consider are controllable in some way. This process often uncovers new constraints. Don't get fooled by the apparently small risks and ignore them – they often become 'project killers'.

Update the project risk log

The project risk log was briefly discussed in Chapter 5 (see Figure 5.4). Some risks become obvious quite early on in the project life cycle, but when you have completed a more thorough examination of the risks, the project risk log must be updated in preparation for the addition of quantifying data from detailed analysis of each risk. The project risk log is not a data document logged in the PDR when completed and never to see the light of day ever again. It is a living document that must be reviewed and updated regularly by the project team.

Risk or constraint?

Constraints in a project are often confused with risks and we need to separate them. Constraints are those things that are imposed on the project, knowingly or unknowingly, that you cannot control and have to live with throughout the life of the project or work around them to achieve your objectives. Constraints may help you bring the project to ground zero and the real world rather than be forced into a 'mission impossible'.

Some typical constraints include:

- available budget and/or cash flow requirement;
- a business critical date when the project must be completed;
- minimum resources required and their availability;
- skills required and not available;
- external resources needed and their funding;
- senior management support and commitment.

Constraints need to be identified as part of the project scope because once clarified, they may require you to amend the scope significantly and that could be unacceptable to some stakeholders. Scope changes during planning or execution may introduce new constraints. Ignore the constraints and you could easily find your project quickly descending into a quagmire of politics and indecision.

DECIDE THE PRIMARY RESPONSE STRATEGY

With your team review the list of risks and separate them into three lists:

- *Avoidance risks* – risks that you can clearly see can be avoided by revising your approach to the project. You may have to revise the initial schedule derived for the business plan.
- *Transfer risks* – risks that could possibly be transferred to a third party for management and monitoring such as suppliers and contractors.
- *Residual risks* – risks that can be managed and monitored within the project team.

These risks must then be listed on the Project Risk Log, using a separate Log for each of the above types. *Avoidance risks* can take considerable time to correct. The consequence could require a revision of the business case, which may lead to more Residual risks being identified. Your primary focus is then on the Residual risks and how these are managed. If you do need to revise the business case then it must be approved by the PST.

QUANTIFYING THE RISKS

When you have derived your list of residual risks, work with your team, using their experience to decide for each risk:

- the probability of occurrence on a scale of 0.0 to 1.0:
  - 0.1 is low – most unlikely to happen;
  - 1.0 is very high – essentially a certainty it will happen;
- the impact on the project if it does happen:
  - 0.65–1.0 HIGH – significant effect on the schedule and project costs;
  - 0.3–0.64 MEDIUM – less serious effect on the schedule, some effect on costs;
  - 0.1–0.29 LOW – some effect on schedule, little effect on costs.

Remember this should be a team consensus decision using all the available information at the time. Avoid the tendency to de-rate a risk through confidence that it can readily be dealt with if it does happen. It is better to up-rate a risk to ensure closer monitoring is carried out.

Once a set of risks has been assessed for impact and probability of occurrence, you can rank them using a matrix with the parameters of *probability* and *impact* on the project (Figure 7.4).

Each risk is located in the relevant box in the matrix by the intersection of the impact and probability ratings assessed. Use these numbers in the matrix to derive a category for the risk and record the results on the project risk log.

		IMPACT ON PROJECT		
		LOW 0.1–0.29	MEDIUM 0.3 0.64	HIGH 0.65–1.0
PROBABILITY OF OCCURRENCE	HIGH 0.65–1.0	*Medium*	*High*	*Unacceptable*
	MEDIUM 0.3–0.64	*Medium*	*High*	*Unacceptable*
	LOW 0.1–0.29	*Low*	*Medium*	*High*

Figure 7.4   Risk ranking matrix

The four sub-types of risks are defined below:

DEFINITIONS

UNACCEPTABLE RISK – Signals a potential disaster. The project cannot proceed without some immediate actions to reduce this risk ranking to lower the probability of occurrence, either with alternative strategies or making significant decisions about cost, schedule or scope.

HIGH RISK – Major impact on the project schedule and costs. Serious consequent impact on other related projects. Likely to affect one or more project milestones. Must be monitored regularly and carefully. Identify possible mitigation actions you can take now to reduce the ranking or minimize the impact.

MEDIUM RISK – Significant impact on the project with possible impact on other projects. Not expected to directly affect a project milestone. Review at each project meeting and assess ranking. Monitor regularly to ensure it does not have indirect effects and turn into a HIGH RISK.

LOW RISK – Not expected to have any serious impact in the project. Review regularly for ranking and monitor. Low risks can change adversely.

Clearly any projects allowed to proceed with many unacceptable risks are likely to be speculative, with serious potential for failure. By identifying such risks in this process you can alert your sponsor and senior management to what you consider may be a safer alternative strategy. Even a significant level of high risks may still be serious and need close management and control to achieve success.

One difficulty often encountered is deciding the impact on the project, particularly during the early stages before detailed planning has been conducted. The nature of the impact could cover a number of characteristics and it is sometimes easier to focus on the cost, schedule and scope, in that order, by asking:

- How does this risk impact the project cost?
- What is the potential impact on the schedule?
- What is the impact on our current scope?

Generally cost is preferred as a more definitive measure of impact since higher costs are related to schedule and/or scope in some manner. Deciding the impact is an increase in cost will help you to decide some mitigation actions that could include reducing the scope in order to maintain a schedule commitment later.

KEY FACT

Risks that do not apparently have an impact on cost can eventually lead to other risks with a cost impact.

This exposure to potential project loss must be subject to analysis to enable effective decision making by the PST when considering continuation of the project.

Record risk probability, impact and ranking on the project risk log.

RISK SCORE

The *risk score* is a useful way to prioritize the risks identified and focus the team on the risks to monitor. For each risk:

Risk Score = (Risk Probability) × (Risk Impact) × 100

Record the score on the project risk log and ideally rearrange the listing in order of the score to show the highest at the top of the list.

WHAT DO I DO NOW?

Any risks ranked *unacceptable* must be closely analysed in more detail. For unacceptable risks you should attempt to reduce the risk score deriving and implementing a risk mitigation strategy with clear actions and action owners to avoid or minimize the risk now. Record and track the actions on a risk mitigation plan (see Figure 7.5).

If any such risks could cause project failure it may be necessary to reduce the level of risk by recommending to your key stakeholders that some changes to the *definition* are considered. No project should continue with many such risks remaining. The PST will want to know that you are focusing on these risks to reduce their severity and impact and that this effort is given high priority by the risk owners. If you fail to get workarounds to make a difference and reduce the probability of occurrence then the project budget will come under the magnifier and the PST will seriously consider cancelling or suspending the project in favour of other opportunities. High risks with a high risk score should be examined to derive contingency action plans and identifiable triggers to signal the risk occurring.

Record the planned actions on a risk management plan (see Figure 7.6) showing:

- when it is expected to occur;
- the probability, impact and current risk score assessed;

PROJECT RISK MITIGATION PLAN		Issue No: 1		Date:	
TITLE:			PROJECT NUMBER:		
SPONSOR:	PROJECT MANAGER:			CUSTOMER:	
NAME	PROJECT ROLE	DEPARTMENT	TEL. No.	LINE MANAGER	
PLANNED START DATE:			PLANNED COMPLETION DATE:		
RISK TITLE:				FORECAST COST IMPACT:	
RISK OWNER:		PROBABILITY:			
IMPACTED ACTIVITY ID:		IMPACT:			
RISK CATEGORY:		RISK SCORE			
RISK TYPE: ☐ T ☐ A ☐ R					
RISK MITIGATION STRATEGY					

RECOMMENDED ACTIONS	ACTION OWNER	Completion Dates	
		Required	Actual

APPROVALS:	DATE	PREPARED BY:		DATE:	
SPONSOR		DISTRIBUTION:			
PROJECT MANAGER					

Figure 7.5 Example content of the project risk mitigation plan

PROJECT RISK MANAGEMENT PLAN		Issue No: 1		Date:

TITLE:		PROJECT NUMBER:		
SPONSOR:	PROJECT MANAGER:		CUSTOMER:	
NAME	PROJECT ROLE	DEPARTMENT	TEL. No.	LINE MANAGER
PLANNED START DATE:		PLANNED COMPLETION DATE:		

RISK TITLE:			FORECAST COST IMPACT:
RISK OWNER:		PROBABILITY:	
IMPACTED ACTIVITY ID:		IMPACT:	
RISK CATEGORY:		RISK SCORE	RISK TYPE: ☐ T ☐ A ☐ R

WBS CODES AFFECTED:	POTENTIAL TIMING:
IDENTIFY TRIGGERS:	PRINCIPAL CONSEQUENCES:

RISK MANAGEMENT ACTION PLAN

RECOMMENDED ACTIONS	ACTION OWNER	Completion Dates	
		Required	Actual

APPROVALS:	DATE	PREPARED BY:		DATE:	
SPONSOR		DISTRIBUTION:			
PROJECT MANAGER					

Figure 7.6 Example content of the project risk management plan

- what consequences are expected;
- the key WBS codes affected where the risk is expected to appear;
- the triggers to look for that signal the risk is surfacing;
- what actions you propose to take now or later if it happens;
- who will take the actions;
- who is responsible for monitoring the risk.

If you decide to change the ranking or risk score of a risk at any time, record the change and issue the updated project risk log to the stakeholders. The actions to reduce the risk ranking may not be taken immediately. Although this is often necessary, the risk owner must monitor their risks and initiate actions when appropriate.

RISK OWNERSHIP

The risk management process is dominated by the essential assignment of an owner to every risk ranked unacceptable and high. Do not attempt to take all this responsibility on yourself; it is important to involve all the team members and utilize their specialist skills. In some circumstances it is appropriate to assign one or more risks to the sponsor or other stakeholders. The responsibilities include:

- ownership for response tracking and monitoring;
- completing the risk mitigation plan or risk management plan as appropriate;
- allocating specific actions to others with necessary skills when appropriate;
- agreeing completion dates for agreed actions with action owners;
- seeking approval of any completed risk mitigation plans or risk management plans;
- monitoring progress with the action plans;

- reviewing outcome of action plans and modifying actions if necessary;
- keeping the project manager informed on a regular basis of status of owned risks.

KEY FACT

Every risk must be assigned an owner to monitor the risk and derive action plans to avoid occurrence.

Successful risk management involves giving the risk owners appropriate authority to do the work that only you as project manager can delegate. Risk owners are often faced with taking decisions that cannot wait for management to react. You are accountable to your sponsor for any risks that you assign to yourself.

MONITORING RISKS

Once risks to the project have been identified and action plans derived, these must be monitored to make sure prompt action is taken when appropriate.

KEY FACT

Because Risks change with time project success is dependent on effective monitoring and appropriate action plans to minimize the probability of occurrence.

Effective monitoring is a key activity towards achieving success. If risks happen they become issues that have a time-related cost impact. Unresolved issues do not disappear, they just accumulate and threaten to drown the whole project. You must act promptly to avoid this happening.

- *Assign each risk to a team member* who has the knowledge, experience and responsibility for that part of the project most likely to be affected by the risk. Stress the importance of this responsibility in relation to project success and avoiding losing effort on corrective actions after the event has occurred.

- *Insert 'risk triggers' in the project plans* to focus the peak period of possible occurrence. For example, if additional skilled extended team members are required in a certain part of the project, there is a risk they may not be available on time. Insert a trigger in the plan several weeks ahead of the timing of this need to focus actions to avoid the risk, rather than wait and see if everything works out as planned.

- *Create the 'Look ahead watchlist'* from those risks listed on the risk log. As the project proceeds you should review the risks at regular intervals and identify those risks that are expected could occur in the next 4–6 weeks. Stress to the team the importance of watching for any signals that one or more of these risks are about to hit your project.

Finally, ensure you continue to look out for new risks and add these to the risk log using the same process. Unexpected issues will still happen and you may kick yourself later for not recognizing the risk in advance. Most risks in a project are (theoretically) predictable but you have many other things to think about so some will slip through unrecognized – until they strike! The power of hindsight is valuable to protect the future.

ISSUES

An issue is a risk that has become a reality and needs to be resolved promptly. Do not assume that issues only happen during the execution phase. They often appear during the other phases of a project and must be treated with equal importance. Issue management is similar to risk management, demanding prompt action plans and effective communication (see Chapter 9).

SUMMARY

Ensure everyone appreciates the need for risk management and understands the process. Spend time with your team to:

- Identify as many potential risks as possible
- Decide a primary risk response strategy
- Quantify all residual risks
- Derive Risk Mitigation and Risk Management plans
- Assign ownership of each risk to a team member

Ensure team members understand their responsibility as risk owners and know what is expected of them.

PLANNING THE PROJECT

Successful planning does not just happen and many projects induce potential failure because of a perceived need to 'get on with doing the work'. Planning is a process of creating order out of apparent chaos, made complex by the environment in which you are operating. Give time to the planning process to avoid significant re-work later. Planning is about asking questions:

- What actions need to be done?
- When are these actions to be done?
- Who is going to do them?
- What equipment and tools are required?
- What is not going to be done?

The purpose is to convert the contents of the project definition documents into a time-based plan of action that everyone understands. This enables you to achieve the results on time, to the budgeted cost and to the desired level of quality. Project planning is carried out to:

- identify everything that needs to be done;
- reduce risks and uncertainty to a minimum;
- establish standards of performance;
- provide a structured basis for executing the work;
- establish procedures for effective control of the work;
- obtain the required outcomes in the minimum time.

Planning is a dynamic and continuous process to enable you to remain proactive throughout the project.

A COMMON MISCONCEPTION

Planning is frequently regarded as just deriving a bar chart showing key activities against time – a form of schedule. This is just one part of the plan. Success with your project depends on a comprehensive plan that contains many other parts:

- a project schedule;
- a work breakdown with definitions of the work to be done;
- a resource analysis;
- a project budget;
- a communications plan;
- a quality/performance plan;
- risk management plans;
- an issue management process;
- a schedule of milestones.

At some time during the project all these are required and each should preferably be derived initially in the planning phase.

WHO NEEDS TO BE INVOLVED?

You and your project core team together. Planning is essentially a participative activity that contributes to team building and creates team 'buy-in' to the plans derived – this commitment is essential to success. Before you start your first planning session, review the skills and experience of the team members. If appropriate, invite experts from other departments to join you, stressing this is not committing them to project work later and you value their input to your efforts. Persuade your project sponsor to attend and open the planning session, explaining the project strategic context, relevance and priority. Consider inviting some of your key stakeholders if they can add value.

WHERE DOES PLANNING START?

This is always a subject of debate and argument. If the customer has an expected completion date, should you fix the completion date and work backwards? Before going any further, some terms we use need to be defined:

DEFINITIONS

A TASK – a (relatively) small piece of work usually carried out by one person

ACTIVITY – a parcel of work of the project comprising several tasks, each of which may be carried out by different people

KEY STAGE – a collection of activities with measurable output, often confined to a functional area

CONCURRENT ACTIVITIES – activities (or tasks) that are designed to be carried out in parallel, ie at the same time

> SERIES ACTIVITIES – activities (or tasks) that are designed to be carried out one after another, each strictly dependent on completion of the earlier activity.
>
> SUCCESSOR ACTIVITY – an activity that follows the current activity in progress
>
> PREDECESSOR ACTIVITY – an activity that is (normally) completed before the current activity in progress
>
> DURATION – the real time in working hours, days or weeks that a task or activity will take to complete – always given in consistent units

Successful planning (see Figure 8.1) is a process of identifying sufficient detail to maximize concurrency and derive the shortest time to complete the project. You start by identifying the key stages of your project. These outputs may be deliverables or interim deliverables.

IDENTIFYING THE KEY STAGES

Two approaches are frequently employed, depending on the size and complexity of the work:

- *Top down* – listing all the interim and final deliverables of the project as outcomes from a collection of activities that forms a key stage.

- *Bottom up* – identifying as many activities as possible and then grouping related activities together to form the key stage.

Both methods are acceptable and successfully employed by project teams. The choice is personal preference. Top down is preferred for larger complex projects initially, followed by using the bottom-up method to identify all the tasks in each key stage.

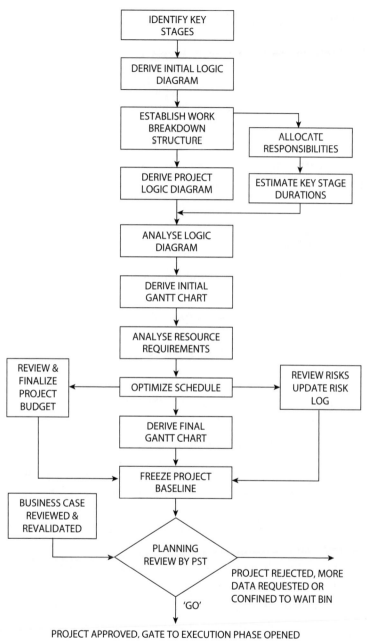

IDENTIFY KEY STAGES

DERIVE INITIAL LOGIC DIAGRAM

ESTABLISH WORK BREAKDOWN STRUCTURE

ALLOCATE RESPONSIBILITIES

DERIVE PROJECT LOGIC DIAGRAM

ESTIMATE KEY STAGE DURATIONS

ANALYSE LOGIC DIAGRAM

DERIVE INITIAL GANTT CHART

ANALYSE RESOURCE REQUIREMENTS

REVIEW & FINALIZE PROJECT BUDGET

OPTIMIZE SCHEDULE

REVIEW RISKS UPDATE RISK LOG

DERIVE FINAL GANTT CHART

FREEZE PROJECT BASELINE

BUSINESS CASE REVIEWED & REVALIDATED

PLANNING REVIEW BY PST

PROJECT REJECTED, MORE DATA REQUESTED OR CONFINED TO WAIT BIN

'GO'

PROJECT APPROVED, GATE TO EXECUTION PHASE OPENED

Figure 8.1 The planning process

Top-down method

Write out the list of final deliverables as defined during project definition. Identify all the interim deliverables that must be produced to reach the point of completion of that deliverable. Remember that a deliverable or interim deliverable must be measurable – apply the SMART test again. This list will become your initial list of key stages, each having a defined output for another part of the project. Later we will examine how these are related to each other, as they are rarely just a set of series activities.

BOTTOM-UP METHOD

Use the collective experience and knowledge of your project team and others invited to the planning session, to identify the work as a list of activities (or tasks) to be done. This is carried out in a brainstorming session. Write everything down on a flip chart and when carrying out these sessions remember to follow the basic rules of:

- quantity before quality – even if the same tasks appear more than once;
- suspend all judgement – disallow any critical comments.

Reduce your task list to a reasonable number of activities, preferably in the range of 30–100 depending on the size of the project. These are the *key stages* of your project from which everything else is developed. When clustering activities, look for measurable outputs again. Do not get concerned that there are forgotten activities. The advantage of using the key stage planning approach is that forgotten activities lose significance for the moment as they are hidden away. You can return to the detail later. This approach generally helps you identify most of the possible concurrency now and gives you an activity list that is relatively easy to manipulate.

KEY FACT

Identifying the key stages is an essential activity and it takes time to do well. Regard it as an investment of time now that could save weeks later.

Using the key stages

Once the key stages are known and agreed you organize them into a logical sequence to maximize concurrency. There are some potential traps here for you: avoid considering real time or dates yet; and avoid assigning people or functions to the key stages. Both will lead you to create errors in the project logic. Your purpose is to generate logical dependency – which key stage is dependent on which.

The next step is to derive the *project logic diagram* (see Figure 8.2). This is done using a technique known as taskboarding. Write each key stage on a separate small card or self-adhesive notelet sheet. Use these as parts of the project 'jigsaw' to build the picture. Arrange them in the right logical order on a table, using a whiteboard or simply using the office wall. This is achieved by taking each key stage in turn and asking:

 What must be completed before I can start this work?

Start with the first key stages that start from a card labelled START. Continue working from left to right until all the notelet sheets have been used. Connect all the notelets with arrows to show the logical flow of the project from start to finish. Some may require inputs from more than one key stage and others may create an output that is used as input for more than one key stage.

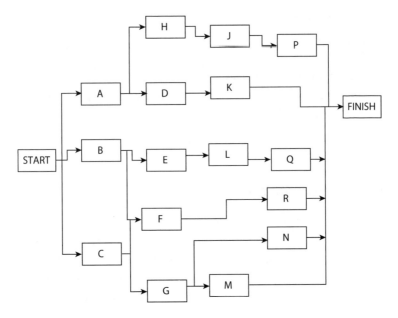

Figure 8.2 The project logic diagram

The advantage of this technique is that everyone can be involved. The graphic impact of the diagram developing makes each member of the team question and debate the validity of the logic as it grows. Developing the logic on the wall allows everyone to see it at the same time.

Checklist Number 8 gives you the step by step process to derive the logic diagram.

CHECKLIST NO 8 – DERIVING THE PROJECT LOGIC DIAGRAM

- time flows from LEFT to RIGHT
- there is no TIMESCALE on the diagram
- place a START notelet at the extreme left of the sheet

- place a FINISH notelet at the extreme right of the sheet
- prepare a separate notelet for each *key stage*
- start each KEY STAGE description with a verb [present tense]
- do not attempt to add durations for the *key stage* yet
- use different colour notelets if appropriate for different functional activities
- locate the notelets on the sheet in order of dependency – debate each one
- when all notelets used, validate the dependencies – try working back
- show the dependency links as FINISH to START relationships initially
- do not take people doing the work into account – can produce errors
- draw in the dependency links with straight arrows *in pencil*
- avoid arrows crossing as it leads to confusion
- label each key stage with an alphanumeric code: AB, AC, AD etc
- do not use I or O to avoid confusion with one or zero
- when satisfied it is correct RECORD THE DEPENDENCIES
- if appropriate tape the notelets down to the sheet then roll it up for filing

" The golden rule of planning applies – always use a pencil and have an eraser handy!

Note that the logic diagram is continuous, in other words, every key stage has at least one arrow entering (an input dependency) and at least one arrow leaving (an output dependency). To assure integrity of the logic this rule must be maintained otherwise the plan will contain errors. Of course it is not unusual to find more than one arrow depicting dependency entering and leaving some key stages.

KEY FACT

Note it is a fundamental property of the project logic that a new activity cannot start until all immediately previous activities are completed.

If you find on reviewing the logic that a following key stage can start earlier than the end of the previous key stage, the latter must be split to show that earlier dependence. The key to successful scheduling using this logic diagram is to ensure you have well defined dependencies.

Label each key stage with a number and keep a record of all the dependencies you have agreed. You may use this information to input to project management software later to prepare the schedule. When recording dependencies only record each of the immediate predecessor *key stage* numbers to any particular *key stage*.

The project work breakdown structure

The *work breakdown structure* (WBS), is a convenient means of graphically presenting the work of the project in a readily understandable format (see Figure 8.3). The project key stages form the highest level of the WBS, which is then used to show the detail at the lower levels of the project. You know that each key stage comprises many tasks identified at the start of planning and later this list will have to be validated. Expanding the WBS to the lower levels is the process of multi-layer planning you use throughout the project.

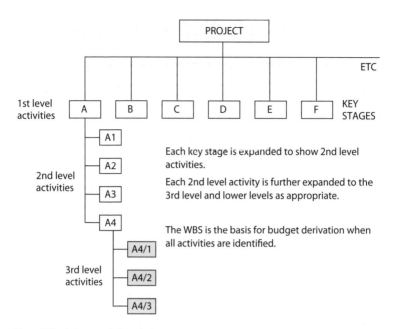

Figure 8.3 The work breakdown structure

Note that:

1 The WBS does NOT show dependencies, just a task grouping under each key stage.

2 It is not time based – there is no timescale on the drawing.

The WBS is normally generated from project scheduling software once you have input the logic data.

ALLOCATING RESPONSIBILITY

Allocation of responsibility is essential to make sure the work is done on time and your objective is to distribute fairly and evenly the work in the team. Each of the key stages of the project needs to be owned by one of your team members.

CHECKLIST NO 9 – ALLOCATING RESPONSIBILITY

The Key Stage Owner (KSO) accepts responsibility to ensure that:

- the work to be done is identified at the detailed task level
- the dependencies are clearly identified
- the estimates of durations are accurate and subject to constant scrutiny
- the work gets done on time to the quality needed
- the work conforms to Quality Assurance procedures and requirements
- regular monitoring is maintained
- regular accurate Status Reports are issued
- problems and issues are alerted promptly to you

A key stage owner can allocate some tasks to others but this does not affect their responsibility for the key stage and its work. You must take each individual's current circumstances, commitments.

KEY FACT

Each key stage must have only ONE allocated owner – multiple ownership leads to confusion and 'no ownership'.

Record your allocated responsibilities

Keep a record of the responsibilities you have allocated on the project key stage responsibility chart. This is a key communication document for everyone involved including the line managers of the resources assigned to the project (see Figure 8.4).

PROJECT KEY STAGE RESPONSIBILITY CHART

Issue No: 1   Date:

TITLE:

SPONSOR: PROJECT MANAGER: CUSTOMER:

KEY STAGE CODE	DESCRIPTION	OWNER	PLANNED		ACTUAL		PREDECESSOR KEY STAGE CODE
			Start	End	Start	End	

APPROVALS:

	DATE	DISTRIBUTION:
SPONSOR		
PROJECT MANAGER		

Figure 8.4 Example project key stage responsibility chart

As the plan develops more names are added as the extended team is identified for parts of the detailed work.

The document is a central record of all the key stages and for each:

- who is responsible
- who should be consulted for advice
- who must be kept informed of progress

As the project progresses, add the planned start and finish dates and identify if the key stage is critical to assist monitoring.

ESTIMATING

An estimate is a decision about how much time and resource is required to carry out a piece of work to acceptable standards of performance. This requires each key stage owner for each of their key stages to determine:

- the 'size' of the task or group of tasks, as determined from measurements and similar earlier work if possible
- the amount of 'effort' required to complete the work based on previous experience

Ask:

- How could the work be broken down into sub-tasks?
- Can it be divided between two or more people?

Effort is measured in project time units – hours/days/weeks. Once the effort is known then optimize the resource needs, taking individual available time into account to determine the amount of effort required from each. Effort is a direct measure of a person's time to do a piece of work in normal workdays.

Unfortunately that person will often have other non-project activities to complete, which reduces their capacity to do the work. At a capacity of 50 per cent the work will take at least double the number of workdays. In practice it takes longer because of the 'back-track' effect due to the breaks in the flow of the work. Effort is a measure of continuous work with no interruptions.

Duration is a conversion of effort taking into account the number of people involved, their capacities and an allowance for non-productive time. Since duration is measured in real working days this is never the same as the schedule, which has to take into account:

- non-available days for project work;
- non-working days – weekends;
- public and organization holidays;
- staff holidays.

The first step for all the key stage owners is to derive some realistic durations and then apply these to a calendar to derive a schedule.

Forecasting durations

As the duration of each *key stage* is the real time it will take to complete the work this is usually the most difficult part of the planning process.

KEY FACT

The majority of projects start with a schedule that has an inherent slippage of up to 30 per cent even before you start the work.

This is largely due to poor estimating. The sources for accurate estimates are limited·

- experience of others;
- the expert view;
- historical data from other projects.

There is no substitute for experience. If similar work has been done before then you can ask others for their own previous experience and adjust the data for your project. It is a reasonable way to start but always take a cautious approach. The equation relating *effort* and *performance* is different for us all.

Who are the experts? There may be a few – or so they believe! Always ask questions about how reality compared with original estimates for some work. Check that the nature or content of the work did not change. You soon discover who is above average at estimating accurately.

CONTINGENCIES

The purpose of contingencies is to attempt to quantify two additional factors:

1 The extent of uncertainty in the estimating process based on expected work content.
2 The risks associated with a particular piece of work.

Contingencies are not intended to cover changes to the project definition or objectives after they have been agreed with the stakeholders. Remember that most people include their own contingencies to protect themselves when asked for time estimates!

Agree the durations to be inserted in the plan with the team. These lead you to calculating the total project time with a projected completion date. Obviously there is a balance between the desired project completion date and the projected or forecast completion date based only on estimates. Somewhere in the middle there is an acceptable solution and only attention to detail and all the experience you can gather will help you to find it.

Time limited scheduling and estimates

Imposed completion dates, given to you before any planning is carried out, always create a conflict. This imposed date forces you to compress estimates to fit the date. To a limited degree this is acceptable as a target but too often this process moves you into a totally unreal situation where you are faced with 'mission impossible'. You must still prepare realistic estimates to derive a clear case and state:

- what you can deliver in the time;
- what you cannot deliver in the time;
- why you can only meet part of the objectives of the project.

You can then use your skill as a negotiator to arrive at an agreed solution!

CHECKLIST NO 10 – GUIDE TO PRACTICAL ESTIMATING

- Schedule full time team members at 3.5–4.0 working (productive) days per week (to allow for holidays, absences, training courses, etc)
- Include management time where appropriate as an additional 10 per cent
- In planning, avoid splitting tasks between individuals
- When tasks are split between two individuals do not reduce time by 50 per cent – allow time for communication and co-ordination
- Take individual experience and ability into account

- Allow time for cross-functional data transfer and responses
- Build in time for unscheduled urgent tasks arising on other non-project activities
- Build in spare time for problem solving and project meetings

KEY FACT

Any estimate is only as good as the base data used and this can change with time as data integrity changes and more information is available.

For each *key stage* keep a record of:

- the estimates you have decided finally
- any assumptions made during estimating
- where contingencies have been added – particularly on tasks inside the key stage
- how much contingency has been added

THE CRITICAL PATH OF YOUR PROJECT

Critical path techniques have been in use on projects now for more than 35 years, having proved their value as a tool for project scheduling and control. The fundamental purpose is to enable you to find the shortest possible time in which to complete your project. You can do this by inspection of the *logic diagram*.

Enter the durations on to your notelets in the logic diagram for each key stage. Begin at the START notelet and trace each possible route or path through the diagram to the FINISH notelet, adding the durations of all the key stages in the path. The path that has the highest number, that is, the longest duration, is the 'critical path' of your project and takes the least time to complete the project. All other paths are shorter.

KEY FACT

All the key stages on the critical path must, by definition, finish on time or the project schedule will slip.

This is where reality hits you – is the project total time what your customer actually expects? If it is a long way out, do not worry yet as most project managers expect this to happen. Remember your estimates are based on people's perceptions. Your objective is to attempt to compress the schedule to a time that is both real and achievable and satisfies your customer. Fortunately another valuable tool of project management is available to help you – *programme review and evaluation technique* (PERT for short). This tool allows you to analyse the logic diagram to confirm:

- the critical path – confirmation of your initial inspection;
- the start and finish times for all the key stages;
- the amount of 'spare time' available in the non-critical key stages.

The value of this data is to give you information for optimizing the project schedule. This tool also provides you with the means to control the project work once this starts.

THE PERT CRITICAL ANALYSIS TECHNIQUE

The PERT method of critical path planning and scheduling is the most commonly used technique for project management control. It is based on representing the activities in a project by boxes (or nodes) that contain essential information calculated about the project (see Figure 8.5). The inter-dependencies between the activities are represented by arrows to show the flow of the project through its various paths in the logic diagram. The PERT diagram (sometimes referred to as a network) is identical to the logic diagram you derived earlier, each notelet for a key stage representing a node.

The four corners of the node box are used to store the four characteristic times for the key stage. These are calculated times using the durations derived in estimating – remember to keep all durations in the same units.

The default or normal relationship used is FINISH to START. Under certain circumstances it is valid to impose constraints with the START to START or FINISH to FINISH relationships between activities, that is, pairs of activities are forced to start or finish together. You can impose a forced delay using a LAG between the START or FINISH of a predecessor activity and the START or FINISH of one or more successor activities. The forced start, or LEAD, is used to start a SUCCESSOR ACTIVITY before the PREDECESSOR ACTIVITY is completed.

Lags and leads should be used with care – it is easy to become confused and introduce errors. Split an activity instead of using leads, to keep the diagram relatively easy to read and understand.

Analysing the logic diagram

The analysis of the diagram is a simple logical process extending the initial calculation you made earlier to locate the critical path. Two steps are involved:

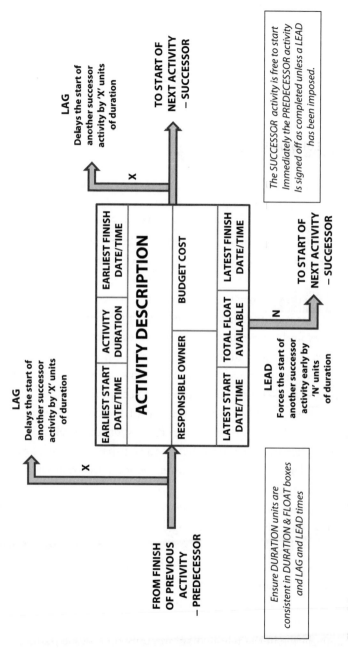

LAG
Delays the start of another successor activity by 'X' units of duration

TO START OF NEXT ACTIVITY – SUCCESSOR

LAG
Delays the start of another successor activity by 'X' units of duration

X

EARLIEST START DATE/TIME	ACTIVITY DURATION	EARLIEST FINISH DATE/TIME
	ACTIVITY DESCRIPTION	
RESPONSIBLE OWNER		BUDGET COST
LATEST START DATE/TIME	TOTAL FLOAT AVAILABLE	LATEST FINISH DATE/TIME

The SUCCESSOR activity is free to start Immediately the PREDECESSOR activity Is signed off as completed unless a LEAD has been imposed.

TO START OF NEXT ACTIVITY – SUCCESSOR

N

LEAD
Forces the start of another successor activity early by 'N' units of duration

X

FROM FINISH OF PREVIOUS ACTIVITY – PREDECESSOR

Ensure DURATION units are consistent in DURATION & FLOAT boxes and LAG and LEAD times

Figure 8.5 Essential properties of the PERT diagram and node box

- Adding durations from start to finish – the *forward pass*;
- Subtracting the durations from finish to start – *the backward pass*.

In this way you and your team can quickly calculate the total project time and find those areas of the project where float or spare time exists.

Using the PERT analysis data

At this point in the planning process you may be looking at a plan that is giving you a total project time considerably longer than you really want. Do not despair – yet! Do not go back and amend your time estimates. The next step is to convert the PERT data into a graphic format that is easier to work with and understand. This is the *Gantt chart* – a very useful tool for project work originally devised by Henry Gantt early in the last century.

The chart is divided into two sections, a tabulated listing of the key stages and a graphic display where each key stage is represented by a rectangular bar (see Figure 8.6). All the rectangles are located on a time-scaled grid to show their position in the schedule. It is useful to have both a project time scale bar and a calendar time scale bar across the top of the chart. This allows you to include the non-working days such as weekends and holidays. The key stages are listed on the left-hand side by convention, in order of their occurrence in the logic diagram (working from left to right).

You will note that the total *float time* is also shown on the chart as a line extension to those rectangles, or bars (the common term), on the right-hand end, that is, at the finish end of the bar. When you initially draw any Gantt chart the total float is always drawn at this end. The limit of total float is the limit of the time available for an activity or a group of activities in series, if the schedule is not to be threatened and extend the whole project. Total float is not cumulative in the whole diagram, only on a single path.

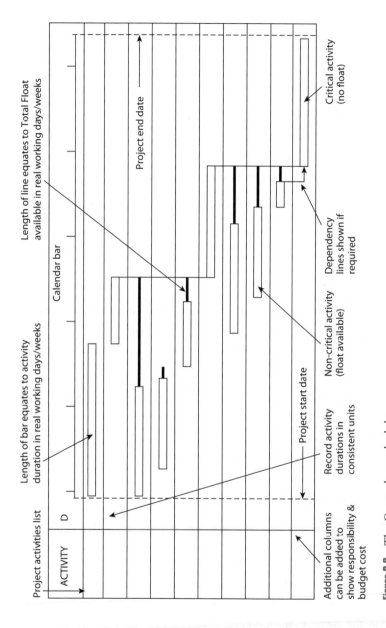

Figure 8.6 The Gantt chart schedule

Of course *critical activities* have zero float and you can choose to highlight these with the use of colour. You can also include the dependency arrows on the chart between the start and finish of the dependent activities (ignoring the float zone). The Gantt chart can also show some other useful information:

- Milestones – special checkpoints usually indicated by a triangle or a diamond symbol;
- Project meetings – indicated by a filled circle or dot;
- Project reviews (ie financial/audit) – indicated by a filled square;
- Key decision points – often called 'gates'.

Remember to give a legend describing what the symbols mean!

 KEY FACT

The Gannt Chart is an effective tool only if there are adequate resources to do the work in the time scheduled.

The Gannt Chart is used to analyse the resource requirements for the tasks in the plan and then optimize the schedule to achieve the result desired by your customer. This may involve 'compressing' the schedule to reduce the schedule time.

Using a computer

The optimization may involve considerable reiteration to arrive at an acceptable solution – a process where project management software is very powerful. Small changes in the schedule are rapidly reflected in the chart and the logic simultaneously recalculated automatically. This allows you to carry out 'what if' analysis, viewing the impact of changing anything in your plan in a host of different ways. You can explore all available options you can think of to derive a finally acceptable schedule.

This process is necessary to convince your customer and the project sponsor just what is realistically possible if clear commitments of resources are made. Obviously this process is much more time consuming manually!

ANALYSE RESOURCE REQUIREMENTS

Ask your KSOs to validate the task list in their respective key stages using the taskboarding technique. Much of the data will have been generated earlier but this now needs some closer analysis, particularly for the initial key stages. Identify the resources most likely to be assigned the work and then working with them as an extended team:

- review the initial task list;
- add to the tasks where necessary;
- analyse for the 'often forgotten tasks':
  - documentation;
  - approval times;
  - testing planning and development;
  - project reviews and gathering the data;
  - project meetings, replanning and planning reviews;
  - customer meetings and user group meetings;
  - negotiations with suppliers;
  - expediting and administration.

Suggest each key stage owner:

- derives a complete list of tasks in their key stage;
- produces a responsibility chart for each key stage;

- estimates the durations of all the tasks in the key stage;
- identifies the actual people who will carry out the work;
- confirm their commitment and availability.

It is good practice to derive the logic diagram for all the tasks inside each key stage. Then determine the critical path and the total float available in the tasks. Some of these tasks may be assigned milestone status later. This enables you to produce a Gantt chart for each key stage. In this way a detailed plan of the work for a particular part of the project is clearly defined by the people doing the work and it minimizes misunderstandings about responsibility.

An advantage of this method is that the detailed work of a key stage does not need to be derived until a few weeks before the work starts. This allows the planning to incorporate any unexpected outputs from earlier key stages. In this way you continuously work to hold your plan dates, seek the required resources, validate your estimates and optimize your schedule to meet the total project time desired.

OPTIMIZING YOUR SCHEDULE

The schedule is always based on the calendar, taking into account the non-working days during the project. It involves taking decisions by consensus to maintain a balance between:

- the schedule – time;
- the resources available – cost;
- performance – scope and quality.

The options available are fairly limited when optimizing tradeoffs between these three to arrive at a solution.

KEY FACT

Float time must never be added to an activity duration to extend the time available to complete the activity

If you use up all the float time in an activity then it becomes 'critical' and the critical path may change as a consequence. Ensure the team understands that float must not be used unless authorized by you. It is essential to retain it for use when conducting recovery reviews and replanning after things go wrong. The options are:

- re-evaluate the dependencies in the logic for the key stages;
- review relationships – initially you used FINISH TO START, now examine if other types give an improvement;
- introduce LAGS and LEADS – with caution though;
- split key stages to get more concurrency;
- review assigned durations – review any contingencies added;
- review original estimates – realistically;
- seek more or different resources;
- seek to get current resource capacities increased – more time available;
- examine to ensure re-invention is minimized;
- reduce scope or quality or specifications – a last resort option.

When you are confident you have a realistic acceptable schedule update the key stage Gantt chart. Check your original project definition to ensure you have not ignored anything – particularly expected dates quoted and assumptions made. Present this schedule informally to your customer and project sponsor to confirm if it is acceptable. If not, then you must seek alternative solutions through further optimization. If the schedule is nominally agreed you can proceed to the final steps of planning before launching the actual work.

REVIEW THE PROJECT RISK LOG

Review all the risks identified during the project definition phase. Ask:

- Have any changed status?
- Are there any new HIGH risks?
- Are there any new risks identified from planning?
- Examine your schedule to identify possible risks:
  - tasks on the critical path (and inside a key stage);
  - tasks with a long duration (low capacity factors?);
  - tasks succeeding a merge of two or more activities;
  - tasks with little float left (where is the float?);
  - tasks dependent on third parties;
  - lags and leads;
  - start to start relationships;
  - tasks using several people;
  - complex tasks;
  - anything involving a steep learning curve;
  - tasks using new or unproved technology.

Prepare new action plans for any new HIGH risks identified or those that have moved up in ranking. Assign responsibilities for day-to-day monitoring of risks to the KSOs. Avoiding a risk is better than a damage limitation exercise later!

REVIEW THE PROJECT BUDGET

Begin by updating the project WBS with all the lower level detail – or at least as much as you can at this stage. This is the easiest way to work out the cost of each based on:

- capital equipment costs;
- resource direct costs – based on cost rates;
- revenue costs for the project team;
- indirect costs – chargeable overheads, etc.

With the costs of each key stage identified you can produce an *operating budget* – the real budget for project control purposes. If it varies significantly to the original *approved budget* in the business case then this variance must be investigated and the conflict resolved. If an increased cost is identified then the customer will need to be consulted for approval. Prepare for this discussion by deriving some alternative options as you did when optimizing the schedule earlier. Keep a record of all costs for control measurement and variance analysis.

FREEZING THE BASELINE SCHEDULE

Review the schedule you have now derived and make sure you have not forgotten anything! This is soon to be frozen as the baseline schedule. Everything that happens in future will be measured against this schedule. You will need to present the plan documents to your sponsor and then the customer for approval and acceptance. Use this checklist to review the plans with the team and ensure you have not forgotten anything:

CHECKLIST NO 11 – FREEZING THE BASELINE SCHEDULE

- Is the *project definition* still completely valid?
- Is the *Scope of Work Statement* still valid?
- Has the Project Manager's authority been confirmed in writing?
- Are all Stakeholders identified?
- Does the team understand who manages the stakeholders?

- Is the *WBS* developed as far as practicable?
- Does the *WBS include* all project administration tasks?
- Are customer and sign-off checkpoint meetings included?
- Is the current critical path established and agreed?
- Are all *key stages* allocated for responsibility?
- Are Key Stage Owners clear about their responsibilities?
- Is the *Project Risk Log* complete and up to date?
- Are duration estimations recorded?
- Are resource loadings and capacities optimized and agreed?
- Does the *Gantt Chart* reflect an agreed schedule?
- Has the project *Operating Budget* been derived and approved?
- Have supporting plans [as required] been derived for:
  - Quality assurance
  - Communication
  - Configuration management
- Does the team include all the skills needed?
- Has action been taken to acquire unavailable skills needed for the project?
- Are the team members working well together?
- Have any conflicts been resolved promptly and effectively?
- Are there any known conflicts with the business plan?

SEEKING APPROVAL TO LAUNCH

You have now completed the planning phase as far as necessary before launching the project work. At this point plan documentation comprises:

- a list of key stages;
- the project logic diagram;

- a project key stage responsibility chart;
- responsibility charts, if appropriate, for each key stage;
- a record of estimates for all the key stages;
- an optimized project Gantt chart for the key stages;
- Gantt charts for the early key stages or all of them;
- an updated and reviewed project risk log;
- a project operating budget; other plan documents as required.

Now present these documents to your customer and project sponsor for signature of approval to proceed, opening the gate into the next phase, launching the actual project execution.

SUMMARY

Engage your team with planning and ensure they understand the principal steps in the process. Work with the team to:

- Identify the key stages
- Derive the initial project logic diagram
- Allocate responsibility for each key stage to a team member
- Derive estimate of duration for each key stage
- Identify the critical path of the logic diagram and derive the initial project schedule chart
- Analyse the resource needs for all key stages
- Optimize the schedule with current known data
- Derive the project budget

Then freeze the 'baseline' schedule, update all data records and seek approval to proceed through the phase gate.

LAUNCHING AND EXECUTING THE PROJECT

You are almost ready to start the project work but before this happens you must go through each of the steps shown in Figure 9.1. Everything is now dependent on the promises of resources you were given earlier and these need to be validated, particularly for the initial key stages of the project.

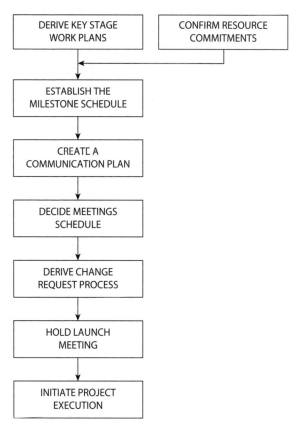

Figure 9.1 The launch process

PREPARING FOR PROJECT EXECUTION

Confirming resource commitments

You have assigned responsibility for each key stage (see Figure 8.4) and it is now essential for each key stage owner (KSO) to prepare a detailed task list for each of the key stages for which they are responsible. This data must be recorded on the project key stage work plans; one for each key stage clearly identifying who is responsible for each task.

PROJECT KEY STAGE WORK PLAN

Issue No: 1   Date

TITLE:

SPONSOR: PROJECT MANAGER:

KEY STAGE WBS CODE:

KEY STAGE SCHEDULE DATES:	CRITICAL ACTIVITY		FLOAT:		Sheet	of	Sheets	
START: END:	○ YES ○ NO							

TASK ID	TASK DESCRIPTION	OWNER	DURATION	PLAN DATES		ACTUAL DATES	
				Start	End	Start	End

APPROVALS	DATE	DISTRIBUTION:
SPONSOR		
PROJECT MANAGER		

Figure 9.2   Example key stage work plan

Copy and send the work plans produced to the people involved and their line managers. This reminds them of the contract they have concluded. The original estimates of duration are only as good as the information available at the time.

KEY FACT

Duration estimates often change as the work proceeds so regularly look ahead and validate estimates before each activity starts.

If the result is not acceptable revisit your schedule and if appropriate optimize the schedule using the same approach as before. Your choices are limited but usually enough to come up with a satisfactory and acceptable solution:

- seek more resource capacity – can individuals increase their time available?
- obtain more resources;
- review and modify the logic inside the key stage;
- amend the scope or quality of the work.

Although this may seem to be a time consuming activity, you are only asking your team to use a consistent and disciplined approach to work planning. You do not need to produce all the work plans at the outset, just those for the first few key stages. As the project continues, you can work proactively to prepare more work plans, taking into full account everything that has happened in the project. This is known as 'layering the plan' as the project proceeds.

The process of proactively doing detailed planning as the project proceeds helps you to maintain the schedule integrity and fast track the whole project.

Establish a milestone schedule

Earlier we showed how risks and issues relate to the project schedule. The milestones are an integral part of this schedule so they are subject to the same risks and issues:

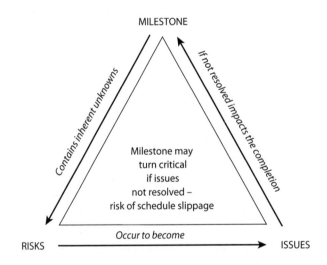

Figure 9.3 Milestone and risks

It is easy to identify too many milestones so remember a milestone is a marker or flag when something significant should have happened and can be signed off as completed.

Some of the common events given the status of project milestones are:

- completion of a key task, eg providing output to third parties
- essential input from a third party
- completion of one of the project deliverables
- stage generation of benefits
- completion of third party significant event, eg acceptance tests
- completion of third party activity, eg delivery of equipment or data
- a financial audit point

- a project audit point
- a quality audit
- completion of a significant stage of work (possibly a critical element)
- a significant decision point, eg abort the project
- completion of a project stage to release further funding or stage payments

KEY FACT

A successful project must reach each milestone on time. If a milestone slips then you must find a way to recover lost time.

The frequency of milestones in a network must be sufficient for effective control through regular monitoring. Record the milestones on a schedule listing and on the Gantt chart. For effective control ALL milestones must be measurable with clearly established metrics – apply the SMART test you applied to deliverables earlier.

Have a communication plan

Poor communication is a major source of conflict so give this serious attention before you start the project work. Ask yourself:

- who needs to know;
- what do they need to know;
- how much do they need to know;
- how often must they be informed.

Establish distribution list(s) as appropriate but avoid generating large volumes of paper. Decide the ground rules you will impose on everyone to get prompt feedback of the prevailing situation with the work in progress. Effective monitoring and tracking of the project is dependent on good communication in the team, between you and the team and your key stakeholders. You need prompt feedback about:

- current progress of the active tasks;
- problems encountered with the work;
- problems anticipated with work waiting to be done;
- technical difficulties being encountered.

Control in a project environment requires you to have a continuous awareness of what is happening and what is due to happen next to avoid hidden slippages occurring. Continually reinforce the need for good communications and create a climate that encourages regular sharing of information in the interests of continuous improvement. Evaluate performance openly; not to blame when things do not go according to plan, but to learn and improve performance.

Project status reports

Your key stakeholders expect to receive regular status reports. Decide the frequency and format of these with your customer and sponsor. Clearly define any metrics you will use and decide just what data you need to receive about the status of the project, such as:

- what has been completed;
- what has not been completed and why;
- what is being done about the incomplete work;
- what problems remain unsolved;
- what needs to be done about these unsolved problems and when;
- what difficulties are anticipated in the work waiting to be done.

An example of a status report is shown in Figure 9.4.

PROJECT STATUS REPORT		Issue No: 1	Date
TITLE:		PROJECT NUMBER:	
SPONSOR:		REPORT PREPARED BY:	
CUSTOMER:			
PROJECT MANAGER:			
PLANNED START DATE:		PLANNED COMPLETION DATE:	
CURRENT FORECAST END DATE:		PREVIOUS FORECAST END DATE:	
REASONS FOR REVISED FORECAST:			
KEY MILESTONES DUE SINCE LAST REPORT:		STATUS	
KEY MILESTONES DUE NEXT PERIOD:		DUE DATES	
CORRECTIVE ACTION TAKEN FOR SLIPPAGE:			
OUTSTANDING ISSUES REQUIRING ESCALATION:		DATE RAISED	
APPROVALS:	DATE	UPDATED RISK LOG ATTACHED? YES ◯ NO ◯	
SPONSOR:		DISTRIBUTION:	
PROJECT MANAGER:			

Figure 9.4 Example content of the project status report

Cost data is frequently reported separately to work progress but budget deviation data can also be included in the standard format if required.

No one likes to hear bad news, but the sooner it is exposed the quicker you can react to limit the damage and take corrective action. You can use this template at any level in the project – the KSOs reporting to you and your reports to the customer and sponsor. Good teamwork is directly related to effective and regular communication.

What meetings do I need?

The different meetings you may need include:

- one-to-one meetings with the project sponsor; one-to-one meetings with your team members;
- project progress meetings with the team;
- problem solving meetings;
- meetings with particular stakeholders – the customer;
- project review meetings with other stakeholders.

All are necessary at different frequencies throughout the project and all must have a clear purpose. The one-to-one meetings are very important to maintain close contact with your project sponsor and the members of your team helping you to:

- know and understand these people as individuals;
- give and receive information at a personal level;
- discuss problems of a more personal nature that impact on performance;
- give guidance and support;
- coach team members;
- recognize their efforts;
- encourage and support personal development.

Problem solving meetings tend to be held as problems arise, involving specific people, which may not mean the whole team. Do not mix problem solving with progress or team meetings as the discussion easily gets out of control and the meeting becomes diverted from the purpose.

Agree a schedule of project progress meetings, throughout the whole project, showing the schedule dates on the key stage Gantt chart.

Weekly short meetings at the start or end of a week are good for small- to medium-sized projects if all the team is on the same site. If your team is multi-site the frequency is likely to be monthly so open other communication channels where appropriate, such as e-mail or video link meetings.

Project review meetings with your stakeholders are less frequent and usually involve you in preparing much more material to present formally to the group.

KEY FACT

Do not hold a meeting because it is in the schedule – if there is nothing to discuss cancel it!

Handling project changes

However good your plans, there are certain to be some unexpected surprises. Minor changes appear during monitoring and are controlled by prompt reaction and taking corrective measures. Significant change is much more serious and needs closer scrutiny. These changes can come from:

- the customer;
- the end user;

- the sponsor;
- technical problems.

All can lead to replanning of the project and scope changes. Any change that is expected to create a replanning activity and affect the total project time as currently scheduled must be handled in a formal manner. Always examine:

- the source of the change request;
- why it is necessary;
- the benefits from making the change;
- the consequences of doing nothing at this stage;
- the cost impact of making the change;
- the effect on project constraints;
- the effect on resource needs;
- the increase or decrease in project risks;
- the effect on the objectives and scope of the project.

Major change can have a demotivating effect on the team unless it is something they have sought in the interests of the project. Derive alternative solutions and examine the consequences and risks before seeking an agreement with the *Customer*. By taking a formal approach to change requests it is surprising how many 'changes' disappear! A major change on one project could have serious impact on the resource availability for another project.

KEY FACT

All proposed changes must be approved by the Customer and Project Sponsor before any replanning action is taken.

Hold a launch meeting

Now you can launch the project. The launch meeting is a milestone in your project after which all project work starts. Collect together all the important people who are involved with your project and explain the plans in some detail. Prepare yourself and your team well for the meeting. This is an important opportunity for you to explain the plan and the areas of high risk to achieving success. You are looking for acceptance from all those present that the project is well planned. You must convince them that with their cooperation you can achieve the objectives. No one can later complain they do not understand the project plan or what you are trying to achieve.

Maintaining plan integrity

New information inevitably comes in to the team members after the work starts. This can be quite casual through informal meetings in the corridor, staff restaurant or even the car park, or through lower level sources in the customer's organization. The input is also intentional on occasions and could have profound effects on the work, the schedule and team motivation.

You must prevent any input amending the plans, increasing the scope or creating more work than necessary and remind team members to inform you immediately of such situations. You are asking your team to keep you informed of progress, so when additional information appears you (and the team members) must ask:

- Where does the information come from?
- Why was it not exposed before?
- Who has decided it is relevant now?
- Is the information accurate and realistic?
- Is there some hidden agenda associated with the timing?
- What impact does it have on the plan and schedule?
- Does this change the project objectives, deliverables or benefits?

PROJECT CHANGE LOG

| | | Page | of | Issue No: 1 | Date: |

TITLE:

SPONSOR: | **PROJECT MANAGER:** | | **PROJECT NUMBER:**

PLANNED START DATE:

Change Request can only be accepted after Impact Assessment | STATUS: Open (O). Rejected (R). Closed (C) | **PLANNED COMPLETION DATE:**

CR NO.	ORIGINATOR	CHANGE DESCRIPTION	DATE RAISED	IMPACT ASSESSED BY:	DATE ACCEPTED	APPROVALS		STATUS O / R / C	DATE CLOSED
						BY	DATE		

APPROVALS:	DATE	PREPARED BY:	DATE:
SPONSOR		DISTRIBUTION:	
PROJECT MANAGER			

Figure 9.5 Example project change log

Project work can be seriously constrained, or even sabotaged by the subtle transfer of erroneous information to a team member. A complete absence of information when it is due to appear can have similar sinister origins. Always be openly prepared to consider changes to your plan when essential. If the information and data essential to the project work are confused by mixed messages from different people then you face potential conflicts and confusion. Prepare your team for these events because they are certain to occur at some time in the project's life – if you have not experienced them already! Establish an early warning system to ensure you get rapid feedback about what has happened and what needs to happen. This provides you with the information to control the project.

THE CONTROL ENVIRONMENT

Control of a project environment involves three operating modes:

- *measuring* – determining progress by formal and informal reporting;
- *evaluating* – determining cause of deviations from the plan;
- *correcting* – taking actions to correct.

Control is associated with the present, so reporting is time-sensitive to allow you to take prompt corrective action. If information is reported well after the event any corrective action is difficult and often impossible leading to a replanning activity.

KEY FACT

Successful control is dependent on accurate and timely information.

The communication processes you established during the project launch are designed to give on-time visibility to significant events.

Design your control system

The purpose is to ensure that you and the team always have the information to make an accurate assessment of progress and keep the project under control (Figure 9.6).

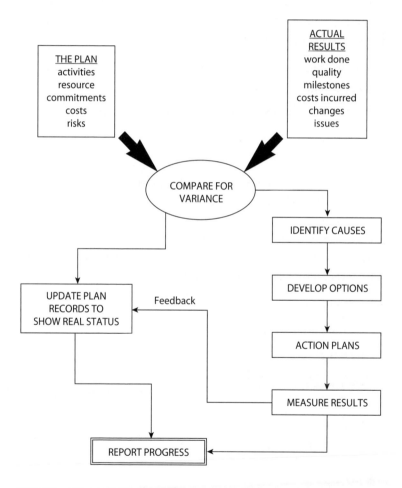

Figure 9.6 The project control system

The best control system is the simplest. The basic inputs to control are the schedule and the actual results observed and measured by the team. The comparison activity should show whether the project is on track and everything is going according to plan. If this is true you can update the project records and charts and report progress and any slippage to your customer and project sponsor.

Corrective action plans are of no value unless you give particular attention to follow up and checking that actions have been completed and produced the desired result. Controlling the project means managing the many problems that arise to maintain the project baseline schedule through:

- monitoring the work – observing and checking what is happening;
- identifying and resolving the issues that arise;
- tracking the project – comparing with the plan and updating the records.

The milestones provide specific control points and the completion dates for these must be maintained with very prompt reporting of any potential slippage to allow corrective action to be taken. Stress that the total float is not spare time and cannot be used without reference to you. Keep the project records up to date with a regular check and update of:

- the organization chart;
- the stakeholder list;
- the key stage responsibility charts;
- the key stage Gantt chart;
- the work plans;
- the project risk log;
- the project issue log.

Using a project management software package can help you maintain your project data – once you are familiar with its many features!

Keeping the project records up to date is an obligation you must fulfil. You could be moved to another project at any time and someone else have to take over. Do ensure that the legacy you leave behind is a good one, otherwise you will continually be subject to queries and requests that interfere with your new role.

MONITORING THE PROGRESS

This is not done by waiting for progress reports to be issued. You need to walk about, observe and have conversations! This is your data gathering process, which if done effectively is far more useful than any written report. Confidence in progress reports only comes from verifying these from time to time. This obliges you to monitor both the team performance and the stakeholders' performance. Monitoring is a checking activity to:

- talk to the team members to find out directly how things are going;
- encourage the team and show you care about them and their work;
- check that promised resources are in fact working on project tasks;
- learn rapidly about concerns and difficulties.

Excessive monitoring may be perceived as interference, so there is a fine balance between the two extremes (see Figure 9.7).

KEY FACT

Regular monitoring with personal contact demonstrates your concern for success and reinforces messages about watching out for new risks or anticipating future problems.

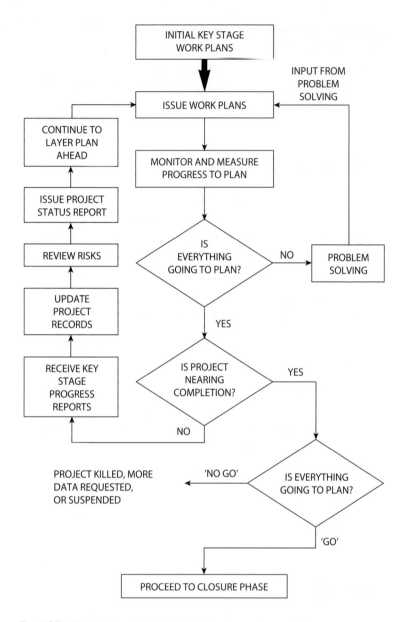

Figure 9.7 The monitoring process

PROJECT ISSUE LOG

Page ___ of ___   Issue No: 1   Date:

TITLE:			PROJECT NUMBER:
SPONSOR:	PROJECT MANAGER:		PLANNED START DATE:
			PLANNED COMPLETION DATE:

ISSUE No.	RAISED BY:	RELATED TO: Risk No. WBS ID	ISSUE NAME	DATE RAISED	FLAG R / Y / G	ISSUE OWNER	ACTION By	REVIEW DATE	ISSUE STATUS Open/Closed

APPROVALS:		DATE	PREPARED BY:	DATE:
SPONSOR			DISTRIBUTION:	
PROJECT MANAGER				

Figure 9.8 Example project issue log

Measuring the progress

Ask the team how progress is easily measured. They must agree:

- the output criteria for each activity;
- the performance metrics to use and confirm completion;
- the frequency of measuring and recording;
- how to report the progress deviations or exceptions.

If unusual or unexpected results appear you need to be informed promptly so that corrective action can be decided. Remind the team to watch out for the risks that are particularly relevant at each stage of the work – these can produce real roadblocks.

MANAGING THE ISSUES ARISING

The purpose of an *issue management process* is to make sure all risks that happen are resolved promptly to avoid and/or limit damage to your project. Generally issues do not go away and success depends on this prompt action.

DEFINITION

An *issue* is any event or series of related events (that may have been previously identified as a *risk*) that have become an active problem causing a threat to the integrity of a project and/or related projects.

Managing issues is similar to managing the original risks, requiring you to keep records of all issues that occur, and ensure action planning is promptly used to resolve the issues. Your concern must be to get an action plan moving quickly. Do not over-react and action the first idea that jumps to mind. Keep a record of all significant issues as they happen giving:

- issue name and source;
- which parts of the project are affected;
- who is responsible for action plans to resolve the problem;
- a record of current ranking;
- a record of when action is complete.

Issues are identified and tracked through regular monitorings.

Ranking the issues and escalation

You will probably resolve most of the issues but some will need the authority of the sponsor. Ranking an issue clearly identifies who is responsible for deriving the action plan and how it is escalated for prompt action. Issues raised are ranked according to their impact and anticipated consequences by assigning a RED, YELLOW or GREEN FLAG.

DEFINITIONS
RED FLAG,

Indicates a high alert condition. A major issue having serious consequences for the project and other active projects. Prompt action needed to implement a decision to resolve.

Responsibility: Programme Steering Team or Sponsor

Yellow Flag,

A medium alert condition. A significant impact on the project and/or other projects. Unless resolved promptly will cause delays to milestones. Automatically becomes **RED** if action delayed more than two or three days.

Responsibility: Project Sponsor

Green Flag,

A low alert condition. Consequences limited to confined area of the project and unlikely to impact other projects. Becomes **YELLOW** if not resolved in time to prevent project slippage.

Responsibility: Project Manager

Outstanding issues are identified when reporting progress of the project. You must also ensure that the ranking of any issue has not changed. It is important to keep your key stakeholders informed on progress with resolving issues, invoking their active support when necessary in the interests of the project.

Issue ownership

Like the risks, all issues must have an owner who is accountable for deriving the issue resolution strategy recorded on the issue management form. Allocate ownership within the team and record all the owners on the issue log. The issue owner must focus on prompt successful completion and monitoring of the issue resolution strategy and reporting the outcomes to you. If difficulties arise the issue owner must follow the escalation process, reviewing the issue ranking and alerting the issue owner at the next level of ranking.

Issues never go away so if no-one is accountable your probability of failure is significantly raised.

Reviewing and resolving issues

The issues are the 'success killers' for your project so it is essential to regularly review all outstanding issues with the team. At these meetings you take decisions on revising issue ranking or resolution strategy, escalating ownership, assessing the impact and identifying any new risks exposed when an issue is closed.

Ensure that you involve the team in all problem solving, calling in additional expertise when appropriate. When an issue is resolved ensure you identify:

- the consequences on the schedule;
- the cost implications;
- the effects on scope and quality;
- any consequential issues created.

Record actions for any Red flag or Yellow flag issues on an issue management plan (see Figure 9.9).

The results of resolution must be recorded on the issue log.

Issues affecting non-critical activities creating a slippage can cause the critical path to move and impact the whole schedule.

PROJECT ISSUE MANAGEMENT PLAN		Issue No: 1		Date	
TITLE:		PROJECT NUMBER:			
SPONSOR:	PROJECT MANAGER:		CUSTOMER:		
NAME:	PROJECT ROLE	DEPARTMENT	TEL. No.	LINE MANAGER	
PLANNED START DATE:		PLANNED COMPLETION DATE:			

ISSUE NUMBER:	ISSUE DESCRIPTION:
ISSUE TITLE:	
DATE FIRST RAISED:	

AREAS OF PROJECT AFFECTED:	KEY STAGE No:

CONSEQUENCES IF NOT RESOLVED:

ISSUE MANAGEMENT ACTION PLAN

RECOMMENDED ACTIONS	ACTION OWNER	Completion Dates	
		Required	Actual

APPROVALS:	DATE	PREPARED BY:		DATE:	
SPONSOR:		DISTRIBUTION:			
PROJECT MANAGER:					

Figure 9.9 Example content of the project issue management plan

TRACKING YOUR PROJECT

Tracking is the process by which the project progress is measured through monitoring to ensure that changes to the schedule caused by issues or the customer are promptly acted upon and that the reported progress data is used to update the plan charts and records in the project file.

Your starting point is the baseline against which the variances are identified. The baseline for all tracking is the project baseline schedule and other plan documents devised and frozen before implementation, when all key stages are fixed. The project baseline should remain unchanged throughout the project. As the work is done you mark progress on the chart by filling in the bars to show the amount of work completed.

If a key stage is late starting, takes longer to complete, or the finish suffers a delay, this is shown clearly on the chart (see Figure 9.10). The original position of the bar on the chart is extend duration beyond total float zone. Baseline unchanged. Project faces potential delay if task is now on critical path unless time recovered elsewhere unchanged as the baseline. Modifications to the schedule are recorded as they occur to enable the experience to be logged for future projects. This may move one or more activities away from the original baseline position, modifying the project strategy for a reason. Keeping the baseline unchanged forces you to fully document any changes to the plan and schedule and later evaluate the key learning points from all these changes that occur.

If any of these modifications cause a slippage to critical key stages then the project completion will be delayed. You then face the difficult task of recovery planning to restore the original project schedule or persuade the customer to accept the extended completion date. Serious slippage of non-critical activities may turn them critical, leading to a new critical path for the project. The critical path is never fixed unless everything happens exactly as scheduled.

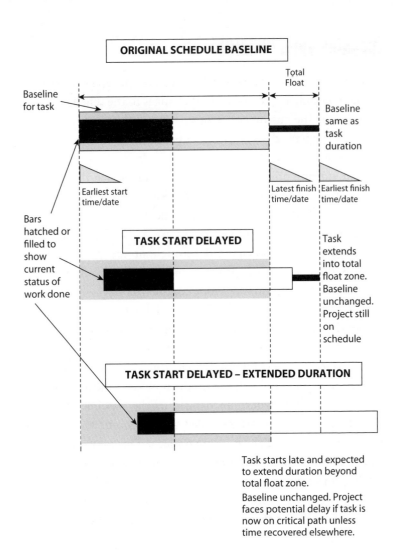

Figure 9.10 Showing progress on the Gantt chart

Define completion

Clearly define what everyone understands by completion. The bar on a schedule is a linear graphical representation of effort. In real life, effort is never linear and depends on:

- the accuracy of the detailed planning of tasks to do;
- the complexity of the work;
- the amount of interruptions to the work;
- the availability of data and equipment;
- how the individual feels on the day.

The well proven 80/20 rule applies – 80 per cent of the results come from 20 per cent of the effort and the remaining 20 per cent of the results takes 80 per cent of the effort! There are nearly always forgotten tasks that take a significant amount of time to complete.

Per cent complete assessments are often quoted in progress reports. These are of little value and you need to know whether the task will finish on time, so ask for a forecast of when it will be completed. This focuses the individual responsible for the work to review other commitments due in the same period and give a more realistic assessment of the time to complete. If the forecast completion date is then clearly unacceptable, take some prompt corrective action. Persuade all your KSOs to get into the habit of forecasting performance for their key stages.

Ensure the progress reports give reasons for any changes to previous forecast completion dates. Encourage the team to develop expertise in accurate forecasting to expose potential future variances. The analysis for variances at all stages must be a primary concern for the whole team, making sure effective corrective action is taken when any issues occur.

Analysis of a variance is essential to expose the causes of the problem. Your primary concern is to maintain schedule integrity – no slippages. Taking corrective action usually has limited possibilities:

- rearrange workload(s) if a milestone date is going to be missed;
- put more effort into the job;
- put additional resources on to the job;
- move the milestone date;
- lower the scope and/or quality of the results demanded by the plan.

Corrective action is normally approached using these options in this order, remembering all could have a cost implication. Record any assumptions you make when deciding action plans – they could have significance later! Before deciding action plans check if:

- the critical path has changed;
- any individual workloads are adversely affected;
- any other milestones are subject to slippage;
- any new HIGH risks are exposed;
- any new ISSUES are exposed;
- any cost over-runs are introduced – do these need approval?
- any localized schedule slippages are controllable.

Progress reporting

Check with your customer and the project sponsor that they are getting all the essential information they need. Avoid creating an enormous paper trail. Keep reports short using templates, but expect to make a more detailed presentation occasionally at a full project review. Focus the reports on the project milestones:

- short summary of progress;
- milestones due and completed;
- milestones due that have slipped;
- corrective actions put in place to recover the slippage;
- milestones due in next reporting period;

- issues escalated and waiting for decisions;
- new issues escalated to sponsor or PST;
- forecast of project completion date;
- forecast of project cost at completion;
- any significant changes requested and actions proposed/taken;
- reasons for any revision of previous forecasts.

Project control is dependent on good communication and feedback. Keep the process working to avoid confusion and misunderstandings and ensure all your project records are up to date.

Progress meetings

Everyone hates meetings but regular progress meetings are an important part of the project control process to review the current status at any time. Take specific actions to make them effective. Everything that has happened before the meeting is ancient history! Remember that time spent in a meeting is time lost to project work. Use the checklist to keep your meetings effective.

CHECKLIST NO 12 – PROGRESS MEETINGS

- keep your progress meetings short – maximum 1 hour
- keep meetings to the point and focused on exceptions
- avoid diversions and problem solving: take to separate meeting
- start and finish on time
- maintain good control – one speaker at a time
- have the updated *key stage Gantt chart* available for reference
- identify the outstanding issues but do not try to solve them in the meeting – set up a separate discussion with the relevant people.
- hold very short meetings standing – no chairs allowed!

Focus the team to expose:

- what has been completed on time
- any outstanding exceptions to the work done
- what actions agreed earlier are incomplete
- when outstanding action plans will be complete
- which milestones are completed on time
- which milestones have slipped
- whether action plans are in place to correct slippages
- any risks escalated to issues
- issues still waiting to be resolved
- any resource capacity changes forecast
- what work is to be done in the next period
- which milestones are due in the next period
- what problems are anticipated in the next period
- any risks that could affect the work in the next period
- any problems anticipated with third party contracts in the next period
- any team performance problems, issues or conflicts – take off line if necessary

Always have a flip chart in the meeting room and record agreed actions on the sheet as they occur with responsibility and target completion date. In this way there should be no doubt in the team who is responsible for which actions and they do not have to wait for the minutes. Avoid:

- long verbal reports of what has been done;
- problem solving in the meeting – take serious issues offline;
- long debates – they detract from the purpose and cause deviation;
- negotiations – usually excludes most of those present;
- 'any other business' – the biggest timewaster!

KEY FACT

The action list is the most important document to come out of progress meetings as this is the starting point of the next meeting – checking all agreed actions have been completed.

CONTROL THE COSTS

The best way to control your project is to focus on cost measurement. To demonstrate success you must not exceed the budget.

Accurate cost control is only effective if all costs are measured, including the costs of people working on the project. This means everyone must record their time spent on project work so that this can be costed. Cost rates often include all indirect costs such as rents, heating, lighting etc for the organization. If the time data is not collected in a consistent and disciplined way, then you cannot control the costs very accurately. Your monitoring process must, therefore, include accurate measurement of:

- the time spent on each task;
- the resources used on all tasks;
- cost of materials (and wastage) used;
- cost of equipment time used;
- capital expenditure committed;
- revenue expenditure committed.

Normally these measurements are made over a specific period of two or four weeks or by calendar month. Alternatively you must resort to applying cost rates to the planned resource allocations. This assumes that what actually happens is exactly as planned. As we know this is not true, you must adjust the costs for each activity based on actual start and finish dates. For effective control you need information on:

- the project budget as fixed in the business case;
- the project operating budget, a cumulative total based on the WBS;
- the costs incurred in the current accounting period;
- the costs incurred to date from the start;
- the work scheduled for completion according to the schedule in the current period;
- the total work scheduled for completion to date;
- the work actually completed in the current period;
- the total work actually completed to date.

The work breakdown structure is the essential budget building tool to derive an operating budget. Then measure costs incurred as the work proceeds and compare with this budget.

COST CONTROL MEASURES

Four essential measures are used for the control of project costs:

BAC – budget at completion: this is based on the operating budget developed from the WBS for the whole project.

BCWS – budgeted cost of the work scheduled: at any specific time the schedule shows a certain amount of work should be completed. This is presented as a percentage completion of the total work of the project at that time. Then:

$$\% \text{ Scheduled Completion} \times BAC = BCWS$$

BCWP – budgeted cost of the work performed: at any specified time the actual work measured as complete is compared with the scheduled amount and the real percentage completion calculated. Then:

$$\% \text{ Actual Completion} \times \text{BAC} = \text{BCWP}$$

The BCWP is the earned value of the work completed.

ACWP – actual cost of work performed: at any specified time the actual cost incurred for the work. The timing of the actual cost measurement coincides with the percentage completion progress measurement so that the actual cost can be compared with earned value (BCWP).

Other terms often used include:

FTC – forecast to complete: a forecast of the cost to be incurred to complete the remaining work. This may be an extrapolation using an analysis model or simply the best estimates of all the costs to complete the project.

CV – cost variance: the difference between the value of the work performed and the actual cost for that work, that is:

$$\text{CV} = \text{BCWP} - \text{ACWP}$$

If the actual cost is above budget the CV becomes negative!

SV – schedule variance: the difference between the value of the work performed and the value of the work that had been scheduled to be performed, at the same measurement point in time, that is:

$$\text{SV} = \text{BCWP} - \text{BCWS}$$

If the work done is behind schedule the SV becomes negative!

The variance measures are often used for trend analysis, because of their sensitivity to changes as the project progresses.

Recording cost data

The simplest way is to tabulate all data using a spreadsheet on a computer to calculate and update the data at regular intervals. Alternatively most project management software includes these standard cost control measures. This makes it easier to incorporate any amendments to the budget resulting from major changes to the project. When reporting project costs clearly identify variances between the operating budget [based on the plan WBS] and the business case budget. Significant variance may become an issue to be resolved. Most spreadsheets and project software include charting features and the data is then used to automatically generate a chart showing the progress of the BCWP, and ACWP against the BCWS as the project progresses. Keeping your own records of costs also ensures it is regularly updated. It provides you with real-time data to compare with financial budget reports issued from other sources.

SUMMARY

With your team follow steps in the launch process.
To successfully execute the project focus everyone to:

- Confirm resource needs and commitments
- Derive a milestone schedule
- Pay particular attention to your communication strategy and reporting and meetings process
- Understand how to manage and record project changes
- Use a control system to monitor, measure and report progress
- Understand the Issue Management process and effectively resolve issues
- Agree and measure the completion criteria.
- Accurately measure, control and report budget costs

CLOSURE AND POST-PROJECT EVALUATION

Finally you have overcome what sometimes seemed like 'mission impossible' to enter the final phases of your project. Many issues can still occur and you must continue to monitor carefully to ensure a successful outcome. Closure of a project does not happen, you must plan it with care and follow some specific steps (Figure 10.1).

Ensure your communication processes keep the sponsor and other management involved right up to the sign-off of the completion certificate. The last thing you want is to become infected with a common virus – 'project drift'.

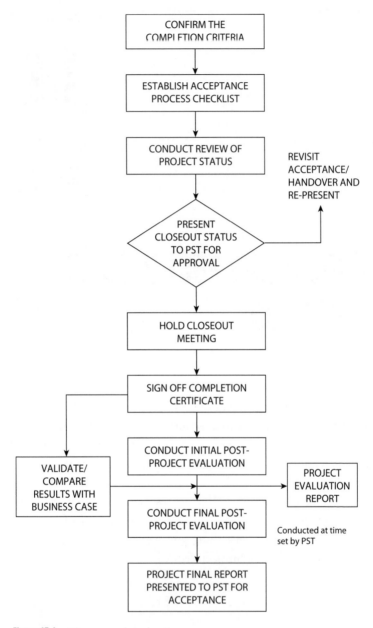

Figure 10.1 Closure and evaluation process steps

PROJECT DRIFT

This occurs when you take the pressure off the control system and allow the customer or any stakeholder to throw in a few add-ons: 'Just before you finish the project, have a look at this modification?' Control of late changes of mind adds significant extra work and considerable costs to the project. This is often when some sleeping stakeholders suddenly wake up and start making a lot of noise!

KEY FACT

Late scope changes create project drift which escalates project costs.

Focus everyone on monitoring costs or your project may become 'endless'. At this time everyone is concerned about their next assignment and this may show as a reduced motivation with a slowing down of effort and lack of commitment. You must keep the momentum going and avoid losing team members to other projects or operational activities.

The customer may experience similar effects too and the users will be anticipating the handover and may attempt to advance the completion taking short cuts. If the new environment the users have to accept at handover are still not popular or accepted, they may obstruct completion and create additional work to cause delays. You can anticipate these difficulties by maintaining good communication with all stakeholders in the closure phase.

SET THE COMPLETION CRITERIA

You should have included the acceptance process in your plan. This will have included just what completion means to your customer and their user group. Check the specific criteria they agreed to use at the outset are still valid. Project completion is signified by:

- all tasks finished;
- agreed deliverables completed;
- testing completed;
- training materials prepared;
- equipment installed and operating;
- documentation manuals finished;
- process procedures finished and tested;
- staff training finished.

All criteria for completion must be measurable by agreed metrics or conflicts will arise.

THE ACCEPTANCE PROCESS CHECKLIST

For most projects it is easy for the team to identify the essential steps of handover. Establish a checklist you must agree with your customer and the user group. This checklist includes a list of activities that must be finished before acceptance is confirmed and could include questions about:

CHECKLIST NO 13 – QUESTIONS TO ASK FOR CLOSURE

- Is there any unfinished non-critical work?
- Have all the project tasks been assigned/completed?
- Have the deliverables been achieved?
- Have all quality standards been attained?
- Is equipment supply complete?
- Is installation of equipment complete?
- Is testing and validation of equipment complete?
- Is testing and validation of operating processes complete?
- Have any required documentation manuals been prepared?
- Are new standard operating procedures written and logged in data systems?
- Are the designs of training programmes completed?
- Is training of operating staff and management scheduled/completed?
- Is training of maintenance staff scheduled/completed?
- Is the setting up a help desk completed?
- Has any necessary maintenance function been established?
- Are there outstanding issues awaiting resolution?
- Have any follow-on activities/projects been identified/assigned?
- Have the agreed limits of acceptability been met and signed off by the customer?
- Has responsibility for monitoring post project performance been assigned?
- Have any budget over-runs been quantified and agreed with the customer?
- Is there an agreed acceptance and handover checklist?

There are many more questions you can ask so use this list as a starter and add your own appropriate questions.

The acceptance process should also identify the customer representative who has the authority to sign the project completion report. In addition confirm:

- who is responsible for each step of the acceptance process and the work involved;
- what post-project support is required and who is responsible;
- what post-project support can be available;
- for how long such support must be given.

Once an agreed process is produced with a handover checklist you are ready to implement the final stages of the project.

THE CLOSEOUT MEETING

To prepare the team for this important meeting hold a team meeting and conduct a full and rigorous review of the project documentation ensuring everything is updated. Check that all work is finishing on time and no forgotten tasks are still expected. At this stage it is quite common to find a number of outstanding minor tasks from earlier *key stages* still unfinished. They are not critical and have not impeded progress until now, so question if they do need to be done. Then agree action plans to complete them and avoid giving your customer an excuse to hold up the acceptance.

Focus on outstanding issues and allocate responsibility for each with clear target dates for resolution. When you are satisfied that everything is under control confirm the date of the closeout meeting with your *Customer* and the *Project Sponsor*.

At this meeting you:

- review the project results achieved
- go through the *hand over checklist*
- confirm and explain action plans for any outstanding work to tidy up

- confirm and explain action plans for any outstanding issues
- agree and confirm responsibilities for any ongoing work or support
- confirm who is responsible for monitoring project benefits
- thank the team and stakeholders for their efforts and support
- thank the *Customer* and your *Project Sponsor* for their support and commitment

Provided you have done everything the handover checklist demands, acceptance should be agreed and the completion certificate approved and signed. You can then plan an appropriate celebration for the team and stakeholders!

POST-PROJECT EVALUATION

Why evaluate?

Evaluation is the process used to review the project and identify: what went well; what went badly; and any variances compared to the business case. Then ask: 'Why?'

What is evaluated?

The technical work, achievements, the project processes and the management of the project are all evaluated. Your success is much more likely to be measured by comparing what is achieved in the weeks or even months after completion with what the business case established.

Evaluation is not to create blame for what did not go well. Evaluation takes place in three modes:

- *active evaluation* – during the project;
- *initial post-project evaluation* – at the point of project closure;
- *final post-project evaluation* – at fixed period after closure.

Each is an important activity and opportunity to learn and confirm that the success sought at the outset has actually been achieved.

Active evaluation

An effective project team is always keen to learn from what they are doing. Promote evaluation by encouraging the team to question the way they carry out the project work. This is particularly valid when issues are resolved by asking relevant questions. What is more important is that anything learned must be accepted and broadcast so everyone can benefit from the experience.

Initial post-project evaluation

Valuable experience and information are gained during a project. At the point of closure the lessons learned during a project should be documented and distributed to all engaged in project activities. Opportunities for improving processes and procedures are often identified during a project when everyone is too busy to make changes.

It is appropriate to carry out post-project evaluation asking in-depth and searching questions about:

- how the work was carried out;
- the processes and procedures employed;
- how you managed the risks and issues;
- the effectiveness of managing the stakeholders.

Remember the purpose of this whole process is to learn.

An initial technical evaluation is concerned to demonstrate that the best results were obtained with the skills, experience and technology available to you throughout the project. You need to focus the team to identify:

- where successes were achieved;
- where technical problems occurred;
- how creativity and innovation was encouraged during the project.

Much can be learned from this evaluation, which adds to the growth of knowledge in the organization. Recognize that your technical achievements may have a value to others, often far more than you can realize at the current time. Do ensure that the technical part of your evaluation report is distributed to anyone who could benefit from your efforts.

Final post-project evaluation

This is focused on two areas of the project performance: a further technical evaluation; and evaluation of business case forecasts. It is important for the PST to get a report at some agreed time after completion about this ongoing performance. Was the project worth doing after all the effort? It is easy to forget the project and what it cost the organization if no performance measurement is carried out.

A further technical performance review is valid to check the results are still delighting the customers. A check can ensure the results measure up to forecasts and that no serious ongoing service, reliability or maintenance issues have surfaced.

The project benefits should be measured and compared with the final version of the business case. All the benefits of the project are not immediately apparent. The results must be compared with the cost–benefit analysis along with all the other forecast benefits that the project was planned to provide the organization. This data is important feedback to the PST and their decision-making process. Although as the project manager you have moved on to another project at the closure, you will almost certainly want to get regular reports of performance over the following months. When the benefits accumulate later, give the team members some feedback – they will be interested.

SUMMARY

Although projects rarely have an absolute cut-off date you have completed the essential steps to:

- Update and sign off all project documentation.
- Agree re-assignments of team members where necessary.
- Issue an evaluation report to the PST.
- Delight your customer.

Now you can celebrate with your team – a job well done! Call a celebration team meeting and ask the *customer* and other stake-holders to come along. Ask your *Project Sponsor* to address the group and put on record the success achieved.

Celebrate and share success with your team, without whose efforts the outcome may have been quite different.

Give recognition to the contribution of everyone involved.

GLOSSARY OF TERMS USED IN PROJECT MANAGEMENT

There is a considerable amount of jargon used by project managers today, enhanced by the rapid growth in the use of personal computers for planning and control of projects. The list gives some of the more common terms and their usual meaning.

ACWP The actual recorded cost, including costs committed, of the work actually performed up to a particular point in the project schedule.

ACTIVITY A clearly defined task or tasks with known duration that together complete a particular step or part of the work.

ACTIVITY ON NODE DIAGRAM A network diagram where all activities are represented by the node or event usually represented as a box. Connecting arrows are used to show the logical flow of the project from node to node.

BCWP The budgeted cost, based on the operating budget, of the work that is actually completed up to a particular point in the project schedule.

BCWS The budgeted cost, based on the operating budget, of the work that is planned to be completed up to a particular point in the project schedule.

BACKWARD PASS The procedure by which the latest event times or the finish and start times for the activities of a network are determined.

BASELINE PLAN   The final 'frozen' plan as signed off by the sponsor before implementation, against which all progress is measured and variances analysed and reported.

BAR CHART   A graphical presentation of the activities of a project derived from the project logic diagram shown as a timed schedule.

BENEFIT   A measurable gain from the project that is a primary underlying reason for the project being initiated.

CHANGE LOG   A sequential listing of all change requests raised during the life of a project with essential information about their handling.

CHANGE REQUEST   A standard template to record and request approval from the key stakeholders for a change to the baseline plan.

CONFIGURATION MANAGEMENT   The practice of maintaining an inventory of system and support documentation – using standardized data formats with consistent units and monitored to ensure any changes are applied across the whole data recording system.

CONTROL SYSTEM   The procedures established at the start of the project that provide the Project Manager with the necessary data to compare planned status with the actual status at any instant in time, to identify variances and take corrective action.

CORE TEAM   The group of individuals selected to conduct the work of the project and usually assigned for the whole project life cycle.

COST CONTROL DIAGRAM   A graphical representation of the actual and budgeted costs of the work actually performed against the scheduled and budgeted costs of the work planned.

COST VARIANCE   The difference between the value of the work actually performed (BCWP) and the actual costs incurred and committed (ACWP).

COST VARIANCE PERCENT   The cost variance divided by the value of the work actually performed (BCWP).

CRITICAL ACTIVITY Any activity in the project that has been analysed to show it has zero float and must therefore be completed on time if the project is not to slip.

CRITICAL PATH The sequence of activities that determines the total time for the project. All activities on the critical path are known as Critical Activities.

DELIVERABLE A specific, defined, measurable and tangible output from the project. Most projects have several deliverables.

DEPENDENCY The basic rule of logic governing logic diagram and network drawing – any activity that is dependent on another is normally shown to emerge from the HEAD event of the activity on which it depends.

DURATION The estimated or actual time to complete an activity.

EET The earliest event time – the earliest completion time for an event that does not affect the Total Project Time.

EFT The earliest finish time of an activity without changing total time or the spare or float time.

ELAPSED TIME The duration of a piece of the work expressed in real, calendar working days – taking into account holidays, weekends, etc not worked.

EST The earliest start time of an activity.

EVENT A point in the progress of the project after total completion of all preceding activities.

FLOAT Difference between the time necessary and the time available for an activity.

FORWARD PASS The procedure for determining the earliest event times of a network.

FULL TIME EQUIVALENT One single person day divided between several persons working on a key stage or task.

FUNCTIONAL MANAGER The person accountable for a function or department in the organization and responsible for the employees allocated to the function.

GANTT CHART A graphical method of showing a project schedule that shows project time, dates, all activities, resources and their relationships. It is derived from the Logic Diagram when it has been analysed for float.

ISSUE A risk to the project, or an unforeseen event that has become a reality and needs to be resolved if the project integrity is not to be threatened.

ISSUE LOG A sequential listing of all issues raised during the life of a project with essential information about their handling.

KEY STAGE A group of closely related activities that can be isolated together as a clear stage of the project that must be complete before passing to the next stage.

LAG An intentional delay period of time introduced between two activities in a logic diagram.

LAYERING THE PLAN See **MULTI-LEVEL PLANNING.**

LEAD A specific amount of time a successor activity should start after the start of its predecessor even though the predecessor is not complete.

LET The latest time by which an event can be achieved without affecting the Total Project Time from start to finish.

LFT The latest possible finish time without changing the total task or float times.

LOGIC DIAGRAM A graphic representation of the activities in a project with clearly identified logical dependencies established.

LRC The Linear Responsibility Chart that displays a complete listing of key stages and/or activities with the names of the resource(s) who have been allocated responsibility for each part of the plan.

LST The latest possible time an activity can start without affecting the total project time.

MILESTONE   Another name for an event, but usually reserved for a significant or major event in the project. Often used for identifying key progress reporting points.

MONITORING   The process of checking what is happening and collecting data on project progress.

MULTI-LEVEL PLANNING   Planning the project at several levels of detail, starting with the key stages and then exploding each key stage to show all the associated activities. Where necessary any activity is further exploded to show further detail of associated tasks at the next level down and so on.

MUST DATE   A planned date when an activity or group of activities must be complete under all circumstances.

OPPORTUNITY   An idea for a potential programme or project that aligns with strategic needs.

PERT DIAGRAM   The logic diagram in the PERT [Programme Evaluation Review Technique] project control system.

PHASE GATE   A specific point in the life cycle when all work stops and progress to date is presented to the PST for approval. Approval at a gate allows work to proceed through the next phase of the life cycle.

PORTFOLIO   The total active programme and project activity in an organization.

PREDECESSOR   The activity immediately prior to an event.

PROGRAMME REGISTER   A sequential listing of all programmes and projects approved as 'active' by the PST. May also include opportunities for programmes and projects under investigation.

PROJECT APPROVED BUDGET   The budget approved at the conception of the project, based on outline plans only with contingency included.

PROJECT FILE   A central file that must contain copies of all documentation, letters, faxes, etc relating to the project. It is the project archive and the basis for subsequent evaluation and continuous improvement activities.

PROJECT LIFE CYCLE   A systems approach to a project where the project is described as passing through four phases from conception to termination.

PROJECT LOG BOOK   A bound A4 book with numbered pages where the Project Leader records all events, action plans and project activities. It comprises a complete event record cross-referenced to the Project File. On larger projects each team member should also maintain a Project Log Book.

PROJECT OPERATING BUDGET   The budget derived at operating level after detailed planning to first or preferably the second level is completed.

PROGRAMME STEERING TEAM (PST)   A senior management committee made up of project sponsors who have the power to prioritize and steer projects in the direction necessary to meet corporate objectives.

PST ADMINISTRATOR   The person appointed by the PST to organize the PST meetings and programme portfolio documentation.

RESOURCE   Anything other than time that is needed for carrying out an activity but most commonly restricted to people involved in the project.

RESOURCE LEVELLING   Utilization of available float within a network to ensure that resources required are appreciably constant.

RESOURCE SMOOTHING   The scheduling of activities within the limits of their total floats to minimize fluctuations in resource requirements.

RISK   An event that has been identified as potentially threatening the project integrity if it actually happens.

RISK LOG   A sequential listing of all risks identified throughout the project life and information about their ranking, probability and management.

RISK MANAGEMENT FORM   A standard template recording risk data and the proposed actions to take when the risk occurs so as to minimize the damage to the project.

RISK MITIGATION PLAN   A standard template recording risk data and the actions required to avoid a risk occurring – usually used for 'unacceptable' or 'high' risks.

RISK SCORE   The product of probability and impact and used for ranking risks.

SCHEDULE   The project plan converted to 'real time' against a calendar by inserting realistic agreed time estimates and resource capacity factors into all the project activities.

SCHEDULE VARIANCE   The difference between the value of the work completed (BCWP) and the budgeted cost, from the operating budget, of the work planned to be completed at a particular point in the schedule.

SCHEDULE VARIANCE PERCENT   The schedule variance divided by the budgeted cost of the work scheduled to be complete (BCWS) at the date considered.

SCOPE CREEP   Adding additional features and extras during the project work that are not recorded and approved using the change process. Many incur extra time and cost consequences.

SINGLE PERSON DAY   A method of estimating activity durations using 100 per cent capacity for an individual to carry out the work. It represents a full working day but in estimating ignores holidays, etc.

SOFT PROJECT   A project where the objectives are only broadly stated and the resources needed are unknown and flexible, the scope left open intentionally and deadlines not defined clearly.

SPONSOR   The senior manager who takes ownership of the project on behalf of the organization.

STAKEHOLDER   Any individual who has an interest or stake in the project at any time during the project life cycle.

STANDALONE PROJECT   A project that is independent of a programme.

SUB-PROJECT   A significant part of a project that is treated as separate for management and control purposes, usually because of size or location. A sub-project is always linked to a parent project.

SUCCESSOR   The activity immediately following an event.

TASK   A specific defined piece of work usually carried out by one person in a finite measurable time. A sub-unit of a project activity.

TIME LIMITED SCHEDULING   The scheduling of activities such that the specified project time is not exceeded using resources to a predetermined pattern.

TOTAL FLOAT   The total spare time possessed by an activity beyond the estimated duration.

TRACKING   The process of taking progress information gathered in a control system and inserting this into the original plan to show the actual status, ie the compliance or deviation from the planned status of the project at that point in time.

WORK BREAKDOWN STRUCTURE   The diagrammatic presentation of all the key stages and their associated activities arranged in a hierarchical format, showing each level of planning.

WORK PLAN   A standard format form or chart for recording an agreed listing of the tasks to be carried out by an individual or department, complete with agreed start and finish times for each within the overall project schedule.

FURTHER READING

Barker, A (1993) *Making Meetings Work*, The Industrial Society, London

Carter, B, Hancock, T, Morin, J-M and Robins, N (1996) *Introducing Riskman*, The Stationery Office, Norwich

Davenport, J and Lipton, G (1993) *Communications for Managers*, The Industrial Society, London

Eales-White, R (1992) *The Power of Persuasion*, Kogan Page, London

Frame, J D (1994) *The New Project Management*, Jossey-Bass Inc, San Francisco

Graham, R J and Englund, R L (1997) *Creating an Environment for Successful Projects*, Jossey-Bass Inc, San Francisco

Lockyer, K (1984) *Critical Path Analysis and other Project Network Techniques*, Pitman, London

Pokras, S (1998) *Systematic Problem-Solving and Decision-Making*, 2nd edn, Kogan Page, London

Rosenau, M D (1991) *Successful Project Management*, Van Nostrand Reinhold, New York

Young, T L (1993) *Leading Projects*, The Industrial Society, London

Young, T L (2003) *The Handbook of Project Management*, 2nd edn, Kogan Page, London

Creating Success series

Dealing with Difficult People by Roy Lilley
Decision Making & Problem Solving by John Adair
Develop Your Assertiveness by Sue Bishop
Develop Your Leadership Skills by John Adair
Develop Your Presentation Skills by Theo Theobald
Effective NLP Skills by Richard Youell and Christina Youell
How to Deal with Stress by Stephen Palmer and Cary Cooper
How to Manage People by Michael Armstrong
How to Organize Yourself by John Caunt
How to Write a Business Plan by Brian Finch
How to Write a Marketing Plan by John Westwood
How to Write Reports & Proposals by Patrick Forsyth
Improve Your Communication Skills by Alan Barker
Successful Project Management by Trevor Young
Successful Time Management by Patrick Forsyth
Taking Minutes of Meetings by Joanna Gutmann

The above titles are available from all good bookshops.
For further information on these and other Kogan Page titles,
or to order online, visit the Kogan Page website at
www.koganpage.com